Optimism is a choice, and in *Trailer Park CEO*, Dawn shows us how to choose it every day. Proverbs 17:22 reminds us that a cheerful heart is good for our health, and Dawn's focus on optimism is a game changer for leaders. She shares, from personal experiences, how staying positive in tough situations has made all the difference in her journey. Dawn teaches us that optimism isn't about ignoring challenges—it's about believing that God is working through them. This book will encourage you to see every setback as an opportunity and lead with a heart full of hope.

Mo Anderson, board member, Keller Williams Realty International; regional owner, Keller Williams Oklahoma Region

Dawn's *Trailer Park CEO* is an extraordinary guide to leading with purpose, resilience, and faith. Each cornerstone speaks deeply to the challenges and rewards of leadership, but the bonus stone on generosity truly struck a chord with me. As someone who has witnessed the life-changing power of giving—whether that is supporting disaster-stricken communities or uplifting those in need—I can attest to generosity's ability to multiply in ways we can't imagine. Dawn masterfully weaves biblical principles with practical wisdom, reminding us all that leadership rooted in service and compassion is the most powerful kind. This book will inspire you to lead not just with grit but with heart.

Alexia Rodriguez, CEO, KW Cares

True transformation starts with accountability. In *Trailer Park CEO*, Dawn powerfully illustrates how surrounding ourselves with wise counsel and holding ourselves to higher standards, as Proverbs 13:20 reminds us, can lead to growth beyond our imagination. As a health coach, I've seen firsthand how accountability fuels change—whether in wellness or leadership. Dawn's wisdom, combined with her deeply personal stories and biblical insights, provides a roadmap for embracing accountability as a gift rather than a burden. This book is a must-read for anyone ready to take responsibility for their growth and lead with purpose.

Danelle Templeton, founder, Journey to Health

Integrity is the foundation upon which trust is built, both in leadership and in life. In *Trailer Park CEO*, Dawn masterfully highlights the importance of walking in integrity, as captured in Proverbs 10:9, and illustrates how this cornerstone is essential for creating security and confidence in our relationships and decisions. As an attorney, I know the weight that integrity carries in building reputations and fostering long-term success. Dawn's personal stories and biblical insights make this book a powerful guide for anyone striving to lead with authenticity and unwavering principles.

    Diedra Sorohan, cofounder, O'Kelley & Sorohan, Attorneys at Law, LLC

Failure is not the end—it's the beginning of a new path if you choose to see it that way. In *Trailer Park CEO*, Dawn unpacks the art of failing forward with vulnerability and wisdom, rooted in the powerful truth of 2 Corinthians 12:9–10. As a business owner, I know that embracing my weaknesses and learning from setbacks has been the key to growth and resilience. Dawn's stories and insights will inspire you to see failure as a stepping stone rather than a stumbling block. This book is a guide for leaders who want to rise stronger and lead with grace, grit, and faith.

    Manecia February, entrepreneur; cofounder, Pigeon Pair Print Studio

2 Corinthians 12:9–10 changed my life. Embracing failure was a game changer for me, and it's one of the reasons I feel so connected to *Trailer Park CEO*. Dawn shows how we can take our failures, our "weaknesses," and let them fuel our growth and future success. I learned to embrace my flaws and mistakes because they're where God's power shines the brightest. This book will teach you how to fail with grace and rise even higher, and that's the essence of entrepreneurship!

    McKenzie Coleman, franchise owner, Christian Brothers Automotive

True leadership isn't about power—it's about empowering others. This book is a masterclass in servant leadership, showing how humility, empathy, and a focus on serving others can transform communities. It's a powerful reminder that the best leaders lift others up, inspire trust, and lead with intentionality. A must-read for anyone who wants to make an impact in their world!

Cynthia Sellers, executive director, Next Generation

Grit is the secret ingredient behind every great achievement. This book doesn't just teach you how to persevere—it challenges you to redefine your limits and embrace the hard path toward success. A must-read for anyone striving to turn passion into progress and resilience into results!

Loretta Tobolske-Horn, ultrarunner and coach, Ultra Crazy Runner; coach, Ornery Mule Coaching; podcaster

Accountability is the foundation of long-term and sustainable success. In *Trailer Park CEO*, Dawn beautifully illustrates how it shapes both our character and our ability to lead. As Proverbs 13:20 teaches, the company we keep and the accountability we embrace determine the trajectory of our growth. Dawn's insights are a call to action for leaders at every level to embrace accountability—not as a form of restriction, but as a source of empowerment. The right accountability partners will have you live up to your God-given capacity. This book will inspire you to adopt accountability as the bridge between where you are and where you are destined to be, both in leadership and in life. Never underestimate the purpose of your life and the people that will elevate you through accountability.

Kate Patulski, president and senior certified master coach, Your Performance People

This book is loaded with golden nuggets of wisdom that I know I'll be coming back to over and over again. I can already tell it's going to be filled with Post-it notes and highlighted lines! I read it in just two days and couldn't resist sharing my favorite sections with my kids. If you're like me and want to live a more meaningful life but need a little guidance and discipline, Dawn has put together the perfect tool kit for you. It's full of encouragement and backed by Scripture, which I absolutely love! This is honestly the best book I've read in a long time. As a creative business owner and a mom, I found this book to be just what my heart needed after going through a rough patch. I highly recommend it to business leaders looking for inspiration and a fresh perspective!

Jessica Smith, co-owner, Anntoine Marketing & Design

One of the most powerful lessons in *Trailer Park CEO* is the importance of creating growth plans. Dawn's insights, rooted in Habakkuk 2:2, remind us that a clear vision is essential not only for leaders but for everyone striving for purposeful growth. As a leader in real estate, I know firsthand the transformative power of written goals and actionable plans in turning dreams into reality. Dawn's personal stories and practical advice make this cornerstone both relatable and inspiring. This book is a brilliant resource for anyone looking to lead with intention and build a future of meaningful impact.

Estelle Ferreira, operating partner, Keller Williams South Africa

TRAILER PARK CEO

12 Leadership Cornerstones to Become a Godly Woman of Influence

Dawn Cazedessus

with Stephanie Katz

BroadStreet

BroadStreet Publishing® Group, LLC
Savage, Minnesota, USA
BroadStreetPublishing.com

Trailer Park CEO: 12 Leadership Cornerstones to Become a Godly Woman of Influence
Copyright © 2025 Dawn Cazedessus

9781424569984 (hardcover)
9781424569991 (ebook)

Disclaimer: The information presented is the author's opinion and does not constitute medical advice for mental or physical health. The content of this book is for informational purposes only and is not intended to diagnose, treat, cure, or prevent any condition or disease. Please seek advice from a medical professional for any health concerns.

All rights reserved. No part of this publication may be reproduced, distributed, or transmitted in any form or by any means, including photocopying, recording, or other electronic or mechanical methods, without the prior written permission of the publisher, except in the case of brief quotations embodied in critical reviews and certain other noncommercial uses permitted by copyright law. No portion of this book may be used or reproduced in any way for the purpose of training artificial intelligence technologies. As per Article 4(3) of the Digital Single Market Directive 2019/790, BroadStreet Publishing reserves this work from the text and data mining exception.

Scripture quotations marked ESV are taken from the ESV® Bible (The Holy Bible, English Standard Version®). Copyright © 2001 by Crossway, a publishing ministry of Good News Publishers. Used by permission. All rights reserved. Scripture quotations marked NKJV are taken from the New King James Version®. Copyright © 1982 by Thomas Nelson. Used by permission. All rights reserved. Scripture quotations marked MSG are taken from *THE MESSAGE*. Copyright © 1993, 2002, 2018 by Eugene H. Peterson. Used by permission of NavPress. All rights reserved. Represented by Tyndale House Publishers, a Division of Tyndale House Ministries. Scripture quotations marked HCSB are taken from the Holman Christian Standard Bible®. Copyright © 1999, 2000, 2002, 2003, 2009 by Holman Bible Publishers. Used by permission. Holman Christian Standard Bible®, Holman CSB®, and HCSB® are federally registered trademarks of Holman Bible Publishers. Scripture quotations marked KJV are taken from the King James Version of the Bible, public domain.

Cover and interior by Garborg Design Works | garborgdesign.com

Printed in China

25 26 27 28 29 5 4 3 2 1

I dedicate this to our kids: Molly, Manly III, Mason, Nicholas, and Micah. I pray y'all—both my girls and my boys—will be encouraged to apply these stones to your lives and become even better leaders than you already are. I am who I am today because God gave you to me as a gift. I strive to be a better person because I know you are watching. I pray that one day my great-great-great-grandchildren will "rise up and call me blessed" (Proverbs 31:28), knowing that I worked hard to change the family tree (Proverbs 22:6; Philippians 4:13).

To my husband, Manly: your unwavering love and support are what keep me motivated to prune every branch in my life that needs pruning so I can bear the fruits of my labor. Thank you for your constant encouragement to keep us moving onward and upward together (Ephesians 5:33).

Finally, to my sister, Brandi, and my brother, George: No one should ever have to go through what we went through as kids, and I am grateful that, through God's protection, we are all on the other side of that life. May God continue to provide a hedge of protection around you and your families. It is an honor to be your big sis.
Ecclesiastes 3:1–22.

Contents

Introduction: How I Went from the Trailer Park to the C-Suite — 11

Part 1: Leaders Become

1. What Makes a Great Leader? — 19
2. What Makes a Great Female Leader? — 31

Part 2: 12 Cornerstones of Leadership

3. Stone 1: Leaders Have Grit — 42
4. Stone 2: Leaders Fail Forward — 52
5. Stone 3: Leaders Create Growth Plans — 60
6. Stone 4: Leaders Practice Discipline — 70
7. Stone 5: Leaders Value Accountability — 86
8. Stone 6: Leaders Communicate Effectively — 100
9. Stone 7: Leaders Prioritize Health — 112
10. Stone 8: Leaders Grow in Wisdom — 129
11. Stone 9: Leaders Model Integrity — 145
12. Stone 10: Leaders Live Kindness (Part 1) — 153
13. Stone 10: Leaders Live Kindness (Part 2) — 154
14. Stone 11: Leaders Choose Optimism — 167
15. Stone 12: Leaders Have Faith — 180
16. Lagniappe Stone: Leaders Give Generously — 196

Conclusion: Final Thoughts from a Trailer Park CEO — 205

Acknowledgments — 218

Endnotes — 220

About the Author — 223

Introduction

How I Went from the Trailer Park to the C-Suite

I never dreamed of going into real estate. As a pre-med student back in the day, I was driven by a love of science, learning, and the idea of success. Real estate ended up being a path chosen for me. At the time, I thought it was my ex-husband who chose this path for me because he was the one who saw the opportunity to join the house-flipping craze created by the 2008 financial crisis. Real estate was something I could do as a stay-at-home homeschool mom to help us earn money to rebuild our lives after Hurricane Katrina. But now I see that real estate was a path God chose for me.

One of my two earliest memories of growing up on the Westbank of New Orleans involved going to visit my new friend and riding my bicycle past a new subdivision being built on the way. I couldn't have been more than eight or nine years old, riding alone one evening—something no parent would *ever* let their child do today—when a newly completed model home, standing all freshly painted and stately, caught my eye. Perhaps most children would not have taken notice, but for some reason, I was drawn to it. I parked my bicycle in the driveway and tested the front door, surprised to find it unlocked. It was after hours, and nobody was there, so I just walked on in, full of childlike curiosity and boldness.

As I turned on the light, I was blown away by the beauty of this house. It was unlike any house I had seen before or certainly had ever lived in. Each room was decorated to make it look like a real home. There was even a little girl's bedroom that was decorated with *Hello Kitty* merchandise. I loved *Hello Kitty* but had never been able to afford any *Hello Kitty* things. As I looked around this dream room in this dream house, somewhere in my young mind the thought came that there was a whole world that existed "out there," and I had just gotten my first taste of it.

I was too young to link what I was seeing and sensing with the idea of success. I just knew that it was a far cry from the world that was my reality: moving in the middle of the night every six months and sneaking our belongings out in duffle bags and trash bags because my parents could no longer afford the year-long lease they'd signed. We were always moving, always in flux. There was never stability. It was always fear, shame, and volatility.

My other earliest memory, however, was not nearly as idyllic as stumbling across that dream house. Instead, I can recall being around the same age and suddenly hearing my mom screaming at me from the kitchen in the middle of the night to grab my siblings and *run*! Disabled at the age of nineteen with a one-year-old daughter, my dad had nowhere to take out his anger except on my mom (and later me and my siblings). As I listened, unable to sleep, while my dad beat my mom again, her warning screams tore through me because *this time* he had gotten hold of a gun. *This time*, he was threatening to kill all of us.

I yanked my little sister out of her bed and lifted my infant brother from his crib next to us, and the three of us raced from the house barefoot in our pj's and hid in the old car parked in our driveway. Locking ourselves inside the car, my sister and I trembled in fear as I held my brother close. My mom eventually escaped out the back door, another swollen black eye visible in the moonlight. She hurried us out of the car, still in our bare feet, to a park several blocks away, where we spent the night huddled on a bench. When we returned home the next morning, my dad was waiting for us, wondering where we'd been as if the entire ordeal had never happened. Today he would have probably been diagnosed as manic-depressive, but we had no idea what that was back then. We only lived in terror of his violent mood swings made worse by a concoction of prescription uppers and downers to numb the pain.

Soon after this incident, we moved away from the Big Easy to the boonies of Bush, Louisiana in search of a better, quieter life. If you haven't heard of Bush, don't feel bad. Nobody has. Back then, it felt like we were moving to the ends of the earth. At the time, Bush was a one-caution-light town, with the nearest grocery store being a thirty-minute drive away. My parents found the only vacant rental property they could afford: a run-down trailer in a Podunk trailer park. In Bush, most people lived in trailers and trailer parks. You could buy a plot of land for dirt cheap back then and put a trailer on it.

One wouldn't ordinarily think of a trailer park in the country as a lifestyle promotion but to me, at least initially, that's exactly what it was. Surrounded by nature, I could escape the violent cacophony of my family life and hide out in the quiet beauty of God's creation. Compared to life in the suburb of a big city, it was heaven. The woods were also a respite from being the primary caretaker of my two younger siblings.

From the age of ten, life forced me to become a high-functioning parent so my mom could continue to commute three hours a day to her minimum-wage job at a physician's office on the Westbank of New Orleans. The job gave us the ability to have health insurance. Starting from the age of ten, I would get my siblings ready for school, cook all our meals, clean the house, do our laundry, go to school, and work at my aunt's day care during the summer. I also worked ironing our neighbor's clothes and cleaning their houses to earn extra money for the family on top of doing homework after my siblings went to bed, playing school sports, and continuing to make straight A's. I would go to sleep well after midnight and wake up each morning at 5:00 a.m. to do it all over again, every day, until I graduated from high school.

Any free time I had, I spent walking in the woods around our family's trailer compound right near the trailer park where we lived for a short time. The woods were a place of peace and quiet compared to the television always blaring inside our trailer to drown out the noise of the beatings and my dad's angry outbursts. I would spend so much time in the woods that I began to wear trails into the earth, paths that I alone had forged. With each walk, I would carefully collect unique and unusual stones to line my trails and separate them from the untamed wilderness. Since my dad was always breaking things in our house, I didn't have anything of special or sentimental value. The stones I collected were my special things. Each one was different and unbreakable. They could weather any storm. Later I would learn the biblical importance of memorial stones in Joshua 4:20–24:

> Those twelve stones which they took out of the Jordan, Joshua set up in Gilgal. Then he spoke to the children of Israel, saying: "When your children ask their fathers in time to come, saying, 'What are these stones?' then you shall let your children know, saying, 'Israel crossed over this Jordan on dry land'; for the Lord your God dried up the waters of the Jordan before you until you had crossed over, as the Lord your God did to the Red Sea, which He dried up before us until we had crossed over, that all the peoples of the earth may know the hand of the Lord, that it is mighty, that you may fear the Lord your God forever." (NKJV)

When I began my firm, 12 Stones Coaching, Speaking, and Consulting, I named it for those memorial stones Joshua spoke about. The name was not only to remind me of my fascination with collecting those seemingly unbreakable stones to mark my path as a child but also to remind me of how far I had come. The memorials in my own life included overcoming abuse and poverty to make it out of the trailer park, putting myself through college working three jobs to make ends meet, and learning about business by jumping in with both feet and failing forward.

In looking back at these memorials of all that I've overcome, I've been able to identify *how* I overcame it all. I've recognized and named the characteristics and traits of leadership I had observed along my way—from peers, teachers, professors, mentors, and coaches—and implemented into my own life to become successful. This led me to develop the twelve leadership cornerstones I speak from and bring to you now in this book.

While anybody can read this book, my heart is to speak to other women like myself:

- the single woman,
- the married woman,
- the divorced woman,
- the single mom,
- the corporate woman,
- the entrepreneurial woman,
- the woman of faith,
- the woman trying to find herself and her "why" for being in this world,
- the woman who came from nothing,
- the woman who feels like she's doing it on her own,
- the woman struggling to make ends meet, and
- the woman with dreams and ambitions she longs to fulfill.

Trust me when I tell you that I have been where you are. I have walked in your shoes, and I want to share my testimony and my twelve stones to becoming a successful leader with you, no matter who you are, where you've come from, or where you currently are in your life. My prayer is that this book helps you take a step onward and upward.

I don't like to say I'm a self-made CEO because I firmly believe that God has been with me every step of the way, leading me and guiding me, and I give all credit to him. But there have been many times in my life where it was just him and me: from leaving home at seventeen and being completely financially responsible for myself, from starting a coffeehouse with no business experience and a $35,000 loan, and from going through a divorce and being a single mom hauling her kids to real estate classes so I could financially provide for my family—to eventually franchising seven successful coffeehouses, being the first female CEO of a surgical hospital in southeast Louisiana, and now being the southeast regional director of seventeen thousand real estate agents at Keller Williams International Realty. I've worn a lot of hats born not just out of a need to survive but from a desire to thrive wherever God planted me in each season of my life.

Today I jokingly say I'm a trailer park CEO, and while it is such an oxymoron, it's also the God's honest truth. I started with virtually nothing and very few opportunities in a small-town Louisiana trailer park, and I'll be perfectly honest, it has *not* been an easy journey. True success is earned, not given. It has taken faith, grit, discipline, endurance, surrender, and sacrifice to get where I am in my professional, personal, and spiritual life, but I see now how God has used everything—the good, the bad, and the really ugly—to get me here.

> I see now how God has used everything—the good, the bad, and the really ugly—to get me here.

It is my hope that, in writing this book, I can encourage you to overcome the obstacles in your life and mentor you to become a successful leader in your relationship life, in your personal life, and in your professional life. If God could do it with me, he can do it with you too.

So let's pour the coffee, sit down together, and talk business.

Part 1

Leaders Become

1

What Makes a Great Leader?

I went to my first leadership conference in the summer of my junior year in high school. It was a huge deal. I was the only person selected from my high school to go because I had been elected president of our student council. It was a huge honor to be chosen to represent my high school at the Louisiana Association of Student Councils, a statewide four-day retreat at Northwestern State University. Nearly four hundred students from over eighty Louisiana high schools were to be in attendance, but there were two problems. The first was that the conference was in Natchitoches, Louisiana, at the opposite end of the state from where I lived. The second problem was that my family was so poor that I could not afford the registration fee, let alone the cost of several nights in a dorm.

The faculty coordinator for the student council wanted me to go and have this experience so much that she helped convince the school to cover my travel expenses. I will never forget how she fostered the seeds of leadership that she somehow recognized in me way back then. She saw something in me I sure didn't see in myself and was the one who convinced me to run for student council president in the first place. I can never adequately express my gratitude to her.

However, I still had the challenge of getting to Northwestern, which was a five-hour drive. My mom commuted nearly three hours a day to work in our only car. My dad was severely disabled and couldn't drive.

They could never show up to my school events or ball games in town, yet for some reason, they both knew this was a big deal. So my mom and my dad drove me nearly five hours away in the high heat of Louisiana summer in a car without air conditioning. After they dropped me off, they turned around to make the five-hour drive home so my mom could be at work the next day. It was such a huge sacrifice by my parents.

I'll never forget the first time I set foot on the campus at Northwestern. It was the first college I had ever visited. I had always dreamed of being the first person in my family to go to college, and being at Northwestern only fueled my desire even more. It made me feel so grown up and smart to stay in the dorms with the other students in attendance.

The conference divided the students into "families" and had us listen to different speakers teach us about leadership skills like how to lead meetings, how to communicate more effectively, and how to work in groups with people from different backgrounds. There were competitions among the families that taught us how to reach goals on deadline. We learned to collaborate and establish a family hierarchy, apply our different skills and experiences, create plans that broke down the problem we needed to solve, divide and delegate tasks, and organize our efforts to complete the assignment on time. It was a life-changing experience. Going to this conference gave me the knowledge to recognize and practice qualities of leadership.

When my parents made the long drive back to come get me after the conference, I remember them telling me how proud they were of me. It was one of the few times I had ever heard them use those words, and it meant the world to me.

Now as I look back over a long career in various leadership roles, I see how so many of the tenets I am about to share with you were planted in me even before that conference. I really began to learn leadership in the years growing up when I played team sports. From playing softball at the Bush Recreational Department to making the volleyball team in high school, I saw leadership modeled to me through my coaches. People will often ask me who my biggest leadership influences are, and while, of course, I look up to the John Maxwells and Dave Ramseys of the world, the people who really taught me the most about leadership were coaches. They taught me about teamwork, discipline, failing forward, communicating—so many of the tools that I will share with you in-depth throughout these pages.

I can remember learning to work hard so that I would never let my teammates down. I learned how to encourage my teammates with words of affirmation if they were going through a slump. I learned to push my team by continuing to push myself. Of course it helped that we were all so competitive, but we knew that we were only as strong as our weakest link, and none of us wanted to be that person. There were so many times when we, as a team, would study together because we had to keep a certain GPA in order to stay on the team. There were definitely several incredible athletes who struggled in the classroom. I would mentor those teammates and tutor them in the subjects in which I was strong, and in return, they would mentor me in areas where they were stronger.

Another lesson I learned is that sometimes you will lose no matter how hard or how well you played the game. In those moments, when it was easy to beat up on yourself and get stuck in failure, our coaches would remind us that it was just one game. They would shift our focus back to the bigger picture, point out how we could learn from our mistakes, and then tell us to train harder for the next game. My coaches taught me how to celebrate with my team and sacrifice with my team. I wouldn't be half the leader I am today without all the lessons I learned from playing sports.

I was blessed to have so much about leadership modeled for me from a young age, and it wasn't until I got into the work world that I learned this was a rarity. Part of what prompted me to write this book was that there are so few books directed solely at women who want to be leaders in business. I could find none on the market aimed at women who wanted to be *godly* business leaders. Sure, there were plenty of books on how to be a godly wife and mom—and don't get me wrong, that is wonderful and greatly needed—but what about the vast number of women who are in the workplace and want to be godly influencers in business?

A 2020 study by the US Bureau of Labor Statistics shows that 52 to 58 percent of families in America are dual-income, meaning that both the husband and the wife work in the business world.[1] Yet the Christian books about workplace leadership are predominantly focused on male audiences, leaving us women to turn to secular books on business and leadership if we want something that speaks specifically to us as women. That realization got me a little peeved. We, as wives, as moms, and as businesswomen, should be doing a better job of teaching and modeling godly leadership principles to our kids. But how can we do that when there are so few resources to model it for us? That's why I wanted to write this book.

You might be wondering, *Well, Dawn, why can't women just read leadership books by men and apply it? Why do we need a leadership book specifically for women?* It's a valid question! My answer is this: I know from my own experience that when I read something that I especially want to learn from and apply to my life, I get so much more out of the reading experience when I feel like I can identify with the author. I love when I feel connected to the author and understand that she has walked a mile in my shoes. Men and women are created differently! We learn differently, and we have different challenges, struggles, strengths, weaknesses, insecurities, and genetic makeups. Look at the vast number of devotionals that are specifically aimed at women. Churches put on separate women's nights from their men's nights so that they can get speakers who will communicate directly to the heart of one sex. After all, each sex can't fully identify with the other because, again, we were designed and created differently.

As a woman in leadership, sure, I have read and benefited from many books on leadership by men both secular and Christian, but I always feel like something is missing. These authors have not faced the specific challenges and glass ceilings that I have faced as a woman, as a mom, as a wife, as someone of peri-menopausal age (and if you're not there yet, you'll get there!). The fact of the matter is that the path to success in business is just different for women than it is for men. This is not to shame or demonize anybody; I am simply stating a fact. I wanted to write this book based on my experience as a female business leader to help other women. I can point out the unique strengths women have in the business world and discuss our unique weaknesses too. This book is for us and by us.

I believe any woman can be called by God to leadership regardless of what you were born into or what obstacles you've had to overcome. If you lead a Bible study or a small group, you're a leader. If you're a mom, you're a leader in your household and to your children. If you're a teacher, you're a leader to your students. If you started your own business or are CEO of a Fortune 500 company, you are a leader. Why do all these things signal leadership?

Leadership is not a position; *it's a lifestyle.*

> I believe any woman can be called by God to leadership regardless of what you were born into or what obstacles you've had to overcome.

But what makes some leaders seem greater than others? Why do we gravitate to certain leaders and find them easier or more inspirational to follow than others? What are the common traits of truly great leaders?

There is a joke that goes, "Are leaders born?" to which the answer is "Yes, leaders are born." The humor is in the fact that leaders do not arrive on this planet differently than anyone else. They are not born with a special leadership gene. *Anyone* can grow up to be a leader. Everything we encounter after we are born is an opportunity to mold us into leaders. However, not all leaders are great leaders. Some leaders can be really intelligent but poor communicators. Others can be driven taskmasters but maybe aren't kind. *Great* leaders are the ones who are not only effective in their giftings or positions but also the kind of leaders that people want to follow. The real question we should be asking is "What makes a *great* leader?"

Great Leaders Inspire Their Teams to Greatness

Think about it: nobody likes the leader who micromanages, is overly critical or passive aggressive, does not communicate clearly, and generally makes the people around them feel overworked and underappreciated. Even if that leader runs a tight ship, is highly organized, and seems to be meeting key performance indicators (KPIs), the whole culture they create feels toxic. People don't have the same motivation or dedication to following that leader and usually will not follow them for long.

On the other hand, think of the leaders in your life who have had a profound impact on you, be it a teacher, pastor, boss, friend, or someone else. They're people with an optimistic outlook, filled with big vision and encouraging words, even when giving correction. Instead of telling people what to do, they ask good questions and inspire their team to think for themselves. They don't view failure as the end of the world but as an opportunity for learning and improvement. They make others feel valued while still getting the job done and, as a result, get better results because the people around them *want* to follow their leadership. It's infectious.

Great Leaders Teach People How to Think

Great leaders don't just tell people what to do—they teach people how to think. I want you to really stop and think about that for a second because it is so counterintuitive to how we learn to lead as kids. Remember back to when you used to play "Follow the Leader" on the playground at recess? One kid was elected (or often proclaimed themselves to be) leader, and they took great joy bossing the other children around, telling them what to do. Even as we got older and began to play sports, our coaches barked orders at us that we had to obey. Our parents would tell us what to do with some negative consequence at the ready if we did not comply. My husband, Manly, is a United States Air Force and Army veteran, and his descriptions of the military illustrate how many of us picture leadership: orders are given, and soldiers are not to question them.

> Great leaders don't just tell people what to do—they teach people how to think.

But when you look at the truly great leaders you have known, the ones who made a lasting impact, they didn't just tell you what to do—although that is certainly a key part of being a leader. They also asked great questions, challenged you to broaden your mind, pushed you to make decisions, and taught you how to think for yourself.

As a parent, one way I taught my children how to think was by giving them choices. Instead of telling them what to wear every day, I would present them with options. That way, they learned to make their own choices, and they couldn't blame me for whatever decision they made. As they grew into teenagers and began to choose their own clothes—and my girls would want to do their own hair and makeup (moms, can you relate to the stress I felt?!)—sometimes they would try to push outfits that weren't completely appropriate for an occasion. Instead of telling them to march right back into their room and put on something else, I would give them a new set of options to choose from.

If they wanted to wear the outfit they were so stubbornly set on, it might have consequences. I would let them know ahead of time what these consequences could be. Depending on what they chose to wear, sometimes they would have to forgo certain activities they wanted to participate in simply because they weren't dressed suitably or appropriately to do them. I would let them know ahead of time that their decision to wear a particular outfit might limit their freedom, but ultimately I let them make the choice and live with the consequences.

Recently we went through some old family photos, and when my kids saw themselves in certain outfits they had chosen for family pictures, they exclaimed, "Mom! How could you let us wear that?"

I laughed and told them, "Oh, no. I gave you choices. You chose to wear that!"

When I homeschooled my kids, my son Mason never wanted to sit down at a desk to do his schoolwork. He didn't love school. All he wanted was to play outside from sunup till sundown. He was one of those kids who was a constant bundle of energy, always in motion. It was physically painful for him to sit at a desk and do school. For a while, I tried fighting with him to get him to sit in a chair and do his homework in a conventional manner, but ultimately we would both end up in tears of frustration. So I decided to give him options.

I realized that it ultimately didn't matter *where* Mason wanted to do his schoolwork as long as it got done. I told him that if he wanted to play outside, he had to do his schoolwork first *but* he could choose where he wanted to do it. Would you believe that his favorite place to do school was crouched under our kitchen table? He would hover over his feet, knees hugged to his chest under the table until he got his work done. As a mom, I didn't understand it, but he kept his end of the bargain so, as soon as he was done, I allowed him to go outside and play to his heart's content. Today we both look back and laugh at the memory of him huddled under the table, but it was where he felt he could be most productive at the time. Even though it was unconventional, it wasn't harming anyone and, in the end, we both got what we wanted out of the arrangement.

Not all choices are quite this simple. I can remember when my daughter, Micah, was in high school and wanted to join every single club the school offered. She even joined the swim team and became the only female swimmer on the team despite not being a competitive swimmer like my older daughter, Molly.

I remember sitting Micah down and telling her that I was worried she was overcommitting her time. I was worried that with all the extra-curricular and social activities she was dedicating her time to, her grades would suffer and she would become overwhelmed. However, I ultimately let her decide what to do. I warned her that there would be consequences if her grades started to suffer and she would have to drop out of some things. As a mom, I certainly worried whether she could handle the emotional stress of all that she was putting on her shoulders. It was hard not to step in and try to rescue her. I wanted to tell her what to do to save her from herself, but I knew that the only way she could learn time management was to go through the process and potentially fail.

Sure enough, there came a point in the semester where she became overloaded to the point of breaking down crying to me. I wanted to rush in and tell her what to do, but I knew that that was not how you train leaders. Instead, I made her decide how to fix the situation. She had to choose which organizations were most important to her and which she had to bow out of—even if it meant disappointing her peers and her teachers. She had to learn how to regain control of managing her time, and she did. It wasn't easy for her. She loved all of the things she was involved in and all of the people she was involved with. She didn't want to quit any of them, but she had to make those tough choices for herself in order to regain a work-life balance as a high school student. I knew that it would be a priceless life skill she would need to develop for when she eventually went out into the professional world where she would be making even bigger decisions in higher-stakes scenarios.

As parents and especially as moms, we want to protect our children so badly that we tell them what to do in an attempt to save them from the hurt of consequences. In reality, we are failing to prepare them for adulthood, when they will have to make endless choices for themselves. It is best to let them begin learning in small, low-stakes situations how to think and evaluate consequences so that when they are faced with bigger choices and higher stakes, they are prepared to make those decisions. It is not easy—especially when we mommas know what is best for our children—but fight that urge to tell your children what to do and start teaching them how to think and make good decisions for themselves. Give them options, educate them about the potential consequences, but then let them make the choices and learn to navigate the outcomes. Don't tell them what to do and take the reins; teach them how to think.

Godly Leaders Know Their "Why"

As Christians, we know that this world is not our home. God placed us on this planet for a specific purpose. Great leaders know what that purpose is. They know why they are here, and they keep that "why" at the forefront of their minds and their decision-making at all times.

Ultimately, our why is to spend eternity with our Father in heaven and to bring as many people as possible with us. But why has God put *you* on this earth? Is it to start a ministry? Become an educator? Have a family? Create a business? Influence the people you work with? Write a book? Only God can reveal that why to you, and in order for him to do that, you have to ask him and be willing to listen. So many people struggle with this. But once you find this out, you're on your assignment. It helps you look at your job as more than a job. Who remembers that '90s TV show *Touched by an Angel*? In the show, the angels were sent on "assignments" to minister to individuals and point them toward God. Even though it is a fictional drama, it has powerful relevance to our lives. The difference between knowing your purpose and following your assignment here on earth is that your purpose is ultimately eternal, but your assignment is how you live out that purpose on earth. We'll talk about this more in later chapters.

As leaders, we can have so much rolling around in our minds and become so busy that we neglect to put God first. But it is only when we spend time daily with God in prayer and devotion and quiet our brains enough to listen to his still, small voice that God will reveal his purpose for our lives. So many people struggle with finding their purpose, and I believe it is because they are more tuned in to distractions and the constant bombardment of stimuli like social media than they are to God. Reorienting focus is one of the many areas where leaders must develop discipline. Discipline, after all, sets up routines and systems that keep us focused on what's really important so we can succeed.

I get up at 4:44 a.m. every single morning. No, this is not a typo! While it may seem absurdly and painfully early to some, I have always been an early bird. The 4:44 a.m. time stamp has special significance to me because the number four is my favorite number. Not only was I born on the 4th of December, but the number four has Scriptural significance, symbolizing foundation and stability. It encourages me each morning as I make my cup of coffee (or Yerba Mate) and start my day with gratitude, Scripture, and prayer before I go on my morning run. My morning routine helps me get my mind, spirit, and body in the right place, setting up each and every day for success. Are there days when I want to sleep in? Absolutely! But I have spent enough of my life establishing discipline to push through those mornings when my emotions tempt me to give in to what momentarily feels good. I know myself well enough now to know that if I give in, I will feel worse in the long run than if I push through that initial discomfort. And I know that when I show up, God will always meet me, whether through a special verse, an encouraging word, or even just a feeling of peace.

Jesus told us in Luke 12:48, "For everyone to whom much is given, from him much will be required; and to whom much has been committed, of him they will ask the more" (NKJV). Leadership is not an easy path, but neither is it an exclusive or elite club. I love how *The Message* Bible translates Romans 2:11: "God pays no attention to what others say (or what you think) about you. He makes up his own mind." God didn't care that I was raised in a trailer park, and he didn't care that sometimes I was the only woman in a room full of businessmen. He saw that I was willing to put in the hard work, discover my why, and have influence where I was planted. And he used that willingness to put me in places where I sometimes had to ask him if I really belonged. If I can do it, girlfriend, I guarantee, God can do it with you too.

> Leadership is not an easy path, but neither is it an exclusive or elite club.

2

What Makes a Great Female Leader?

According to an article in *Forbes*, the percentage of women CEOs of Fortune 500 companies finally broke into the double digits, rising from 8 percent to 10 percent in 2023.[2] Also in 2023, there were only twenty-five women occupying seats in the US Senate.[3] And despite the fact that more than 56 percent of all PhD and Master's degrees were earned by women in the last twelve years in the US,[4] we still see very few women—less than 25 percent—in leadership positions in STEM categories.[5]

So why aren't there more great female leaders? Judging by these statistics, the answer is not that women aren't smart enough or qualified enough, nor is it that they lack access to education or positions of influence. There are so many opportunities for women today—way more than there were one hundred years ago, when women first got the right to vote, or even fifty years ago, when I was growing up and watched my mom struggle to support three children and a disabled husband while limited to secretarial work with no chance for upward mobility. Times have definitely changed for the better in this respect.

Now don't get me wrong: this is not going to be a chapter that denigrates men or blames men in order to lift women up. That's not the way I do things. As a mom of both sons and daughters, I want to equip them all for success regardless of their gender, and I firmly subscribe to what the Bible says in Genesis 1:27: "God created man in His own image; He created him in the image of God; He created them male and female" (HCSB).

God created both men and women in his holy image, and he has gifted men and women with different talents and characteristics that complement each other. God even used both men and women in the Bible to lead and have influence. Think about Esther. Talk about influence—she saved the entire Hebrew race! However, in order for women to succeed as leaders today in a predominantly male-dominated workforce, we need to be aware of our strengths and weaknesses so we can lean into our God-given strengths and work to overcome weaknesses.

As I already established in the last chapter, great leaders don't tell others what to do but teach them how to think. So I am going to give you some things to think about that will help you, especially as women, to reframe the way you look at leadership. There are certain characteristics I have learned and other traits I've had to overcome in my lifetime to become a leader, and through this book, I want to equip and empower you to stand out as female leaders.

Keeping Emotions Between the Lines

One thing I admire about pilots is that they always sound calm when they speak over the intercom. Whether facing turbulence or something more serious, a pilot's ability to keep their emotions in check goes a long way toward making their passengers confident they will land the aircraft safely.

If you've ever listened to the tapes of Captain "Sully" Sullenberger when he had to make an emergency landing on the Hudson River back in 2009, you may remember that his voice never betrayed the stress he was feeling.[6] His voice on the airplane's cockpit recordings sounds like a late-night drive-time DJ. Granted, this is an extreme example of keeping emotions under control, but the principle of calmness involved is valuable for other situations of life.

As women, we are inherently emotional beings, and it can sometimes be difficult for us to keep our emotions in check, especially in the workplace. Part of it is our hormones, but part of it is that, as nurturers and caretakers, we are in tune to the needs and emotions of others. It's why we're the child-bearers and child-raisers. It comes from our DNA, our body chemistry, and the way our brains are wired. It's how God quite literally designed and crafted us. But in business, emotions can often be a detriment to women. We can be naturally more empathetic than men and more personally invested in both the well-being of other people and situational outcomes. This can cause our emotions to be pulled into scenarios and cloud our objective reasoning and judgment. It can make us seem unstable, which is why women who are great leaders are not overly emotional or demonstrative. They have the ability to keep their emotions between the lines because they have practiced it time and time again and developed a high level of control.

In the 1990s, emotional intelligence (EQ) became a popular research and conversation topic and continues to be discussed today, especially in workplace scenarios. EQ is the ability to be aware of one's own emotions and to control them.[7] While a lot of women are self-aware and able to recognize and communicate the emotions they are feeling, I have observed that where we struggle with EQ is in keeping our emotions between the lines.

These lines provide safe boundaries and guidelines for us and for others, just like the road lines we keep our car between when we drive. As leaders tasked with many responsibilities and teams of people following us, we cannot be overly emotional because that creates distrust and insecurity around us. As an employee, you don't want to be constantly wondering how the person in charge is feeling and if you have to adjust your performance or walk on eggshells to accommodate their ever-changing moods. You want the person at the helm to be stable, unflappable, rock-solid, and consistent.

This does not mean that women should ignore or stuff their emotions, but it means that we must learn how and when to control them. The workplace is not the right environment for emotional outbursts if we're trying to prove we can handle the pressure of a higher-stress position or if we're negotiating conflict between high-powered individuals that could drastically affect the productivity and direction of a department or company. Keeping our emotions between the lines shows self-control and self-awareness, and it demonstrates to those around us that they can trust us to get through difficult situations.

> Keeping our emotions between the lines shows self-control and self-awareness, and it demonstrates to those around us that they can trust us to get through difficult situations.

Enduring the Pain Cave

Another reason why we're seeing more women in leadership and in C-suites than ever before is because we are recognizing in companies that those who have higher EQ can foster a spirit of teamwork and collaboration. Women will naturally bring community to the workplace whereas men, in my experience, often think, *I have to do everything by myself.* Men are great fixers. They see a problem and immediately look for ways to solve it. They actually enjoy the challenge of finding solutions. However, in their eagerness to fix things, they can sometimes forget to pause to recognize the symptoms or root causes behind a problem. Women, on the other hand, shine at digging deeper. Because women want to do things together and will look for ways to build relationships in the workplace and encourage each other, they are willing to have the more difficult conversations when conflicts arise. They want to understand *why* people are upset rather than just rush to fix a problem. They seek to understand the root causes behind the resulting symptoms, and this sets the expectation that everyone will make it through difficult times (what I sometimes call "the pain cave") together.

I was listening to an ultrarunning[8] podcast the other day (because I have gotten into the ultrarunning and ultramarathon community; I'm training for a fifty-miler for my fiftieth birthday this year), and the podcast said that women have higher endurance and higher pain tolerance than men. It's funny that not even sixty years ago, women were prevented from running marathon distances because men thought that our uteruses would fall out.

When Roberta Gibb heard this, she said it was her mission to prove them wrong, and in 1966, she became the first woman to unofficially run the Boston Marathon. She had to dress up as a man and register as a male under the name of Bobbi Gibb in order to run. She cut her hair short, and instead of wearing the racing tank and shorts, she wore a sweatshirt to cover up her body. Once the race officials figured out that she was really a woman, they chased her down and tried to pull her out of the race, but the other male runners protected her and fended off the officials so she could finish.[9]

Even though she finished the race, her time was officially disqualified, and it wasn't accepted until 1967, when Kathrine Fisher became the first official female marathon runner.[10] It still took an additional five years for officials to open the Boston Marathon to women participants.[11]

But when you really think about it, it's not so difficult to believe that women are able to run such long distances without stopping or quitting. Think about what women have had to fight for just in the last century: the right to own property without a husband in 1900, the right to vote in 1920, the right to equal pay in 1963[12] (and women still struggle today to earn only 84 percent of what their male counterparts do),[13] and the ability to open bank accounts in their own names in 1974.[14] Not to mention enduring the pain of childbirth, for which women were not allowed to use epidurals until the 1960s, and even that didn't become commonplace until the 1970s.[15]

For so long, women have had to overcome and endure many obstacles, fighting for their right to a seat at the table in ways that men have never faced. Again, this is nothing against men. But women have had to develop grit, endurance, and long-suffering to make it to the C-suite. We've had to balance more responsibilities—such as marriage, kids, housework, social engagements, and faith—while handling our work responsibilities. We have formed support groups and communities where we can rely on each other to stay motivated in difficult times. We don't have to fear going through things alone because we know other women who have gone before us, are alongside us, and will encourage us to keep going in the midst of the struggle.

But let's go back to ultrarunning for a minute, because there is a really important point that I want to make and that I, myself, have experienced since I first got involved in this incredible community: women can stay in the pain cave longer than men can.

In ultrarunning, the pain cave is a psychological and physiological state of being where "muscles ache, the lactic acid builds, and you slip into oxygen debt."[16] It inevitably happens, no matter how hard you've mentally and physically prepared for it. Hour after hour, mile after mile, you don't know when (or if) the all-consuming pain will end. We are tempted to quit; it becomes difficult to stay on pace and on course while our emotions, our body, and our mind betray us.

Yet every experienced runner knows that the pain cave is just a phase. It will end. The pain will subside. You just have to keep moving through it. But I've noticed in my experience with ultramarathons, women come out of the pain cave stronger—less emotionally, mentally, and physically beat down than men. We are able to grit our teeth and endure a higher level of pain and discomfort both as athletes and as businesswomen.

> The pain cave is just a phase. It will end. The pain will subside. You just have to keep moving through it.

One of my ultrarunning heroes, Courtney Dauwalter, says that she tells herself, "It's not always going to feel great, but that's going to make us better. We're going to get better from visiting it."[17] Courtney will visualize her pain cave and set small goals for herself to keep going just one more mile after just one more mile until she makes it through the pain cave and can finish her race. She doesn't think about her race performance in such polarizing terms such as "wins" and "failures." She reframes the binary and thinks about it instead as a learning experience where the things that did not serve her well are left by the wayside and replaced with new techniques to try. She does not let the pain cave stop her from always moving forward, and female leaders have exhibited this same "onward and upward" approach to enduring and overcoming obstacles and glass ceilings in life and business.

Becoming Comfortable with Change

The third area that sets great female leaders apart is in becoming comfortable with change and being able to make decisions in the midst of change. You know the old adage "The only constant in life is change"? It is so true. Women tend to struggle with this because we seek stability and safety, but to become great leaders, we have to accept that life is change and business is change.

Since I entered the real estate market in 2008, I have had to navigate the 2008 recession, multiple hurricanes and tornadoes, fluctuating interest rates, a global pandemic, and now, legislation that is massively changing the real estate industry. Of course there is the temptation each time to throw up my hands and say, *Really?* But markets and industries are always going to be changing, and if you want to lead, you have to be willing to change with the times and trends.

Generally speaking, I have noticed that men deal with these changes better than women. Yes, there are always exceptions, but typically men's brains seem more naturally wired to embrace change, take bigger risks, and make decisions more efficiently. This is not to say that women can't learn to do these things, but I have continually seen women struggle in these areas in the workplace and get passed up for promotions time and time again as a result. I see women get stuck because they overwhelm themselves with data analysis and fall into "analysis paralysis," so afraid of making a wrong decision that they put off making any decision at all. Where great women leaders set themselves apart is in their ability to roll with the changing tides and still make decisions.

When Courtney Dauwalter stopped attaching the "failure" label to her running performance, she was able to learn from her mistakes. Let me tell you right now, if you are a woman in leadership, you are going to make mistakes. It is unavoidable. Mistakes are not the end of the world. Failure is not the end of the world. The best leaders have all failed on their way to the top. Some have failed in very big and very public ways. But they did not let it stop them from ever making a decision again. As soon as you can get comfortable with reframing failure as an opportunity for growth and improvement, you can take some of the fear away from making decisions. When I have big decisions to make that seem overwhelming to me, I cling tightly to Romans 8:26–30:

> In the same way the Spirit also joins to help in our weakness, because we do not know what to pray for as we should, but the Spirit Himself intercedes for us with unspoken groanings. And He who searches the hearts knows the Spirit's mind-set, because He intercedes for the saints according to the will of God. We know that all things work together for the good of those who love God: those who are called according to His purpose. For those He foreknew He also predestined to be conformed to the image of His Son, so that He would be the firstborn among many brothers. And those He predestined, He

also called; and those He called, He also justified; and those He justified, He also glorified. (HCSB)

I find such comfort from this passage because God tells us that his Holy Spirit will make up for our shortcomings. He intercedes for us and has *predestined* us to his purpose. We're already justified and glorified in him. I can trust that if I make a wrong decision, God will help make it right.

In the secular world, many women will talk about following their gut feeling when making big business decisions because they don't have the knowledge of the Holy Spirit guiding them. We, as Christians, do! That should give us so much freedom to know that God is standing in the gap for us. He knows all the changes we are going to face before we face them because he has already written our story. Sometimes he will take us through the pain cave, and sometimes it will be harder than others to keep our emotions between the lines, but we can have faith knowing that God will guide us through the changes (both good and bad), help us make the best decisions we can make, and get us back on track, whatever the outcome.

The entire purpose of this book is to equip women with the tools they will need to become successful leaders and grow their influence in life and in business. Even if you're not a businesswoman or you don't think you are "leadership" material, you can still have influence. You can be a leader in your family, your friend group, or your church. You can be a leader for a particular season or purpose. This is the book that I wish I could have had when I was starting out in life. This is the book I want my daughters to read and apply so God can use and bless them even more mightily than he has used and blessed me.

When I was starting out in my career, I didn't have a clue what I was doing. I had not had success modeled to me in my early life. I didn't know what leadership looked like in a business setting. If you have read the introduction to this book, you already know! (If you skipped the introduction, hit pause and go take a look. I'll take a second to rewarm my coffee.) I relied heavily on observing the leaders around me, reading books by secular businessmen, and attending leadership seminars—any resource I could find that would teach me how to become a better leader.

Along the way, I began compiling a list of traits that I noticed were common to the leaders I admired until I had what I now call my "twelve stones of leadership." In this book, I will share with you the twelve stones that have helped me go from the trailer park to the C-suite and build my sphere of influence as a leader. In addition to the twelve major stones, I will break each one of those core tenets into smaller "stepping stones" that are designed to get you thinking about how you can make changes in your life and give you practical tools to start applying them. Let's jump in!

Part 2

12 Cornerstones of Leadership

3

Stone 1: Leaders Have Grit

It's 4:44 a.m. My alarm goes off. Not even the sun is awake yet, but I am. I don't necessarily *want* to be. My body would love to stay under the blankets longer, but I get out of bed, stretch, and go to fix a cup of fresh coffee. I start my day with devotions and gratitude journaling as I wait for the coffee to brew. The smell of my special blend, reminiscent of the days when I owned my own coffee franchise, Mochaccinos, helps my brain wake up even before that first comforting sip. I enjoy a few minutes of quiet reflection and prayer before I lace up my running shoes.

Today is going to be a difficult run as I train for the fifty-mile ultramarathon I set as a goal to celebrate turning fifty this year. I have twelve miles to run today through the trails of North Atlanta, up and down hills that my body, coming from the flat swamplands of southeast Louisiana, is not used to.

I step outside and…it's raining. Not just a light drizzle. It is pouring. There is thunder and lightning in the distance. I have a decision to make. I can start making excuses, or I can grit my way through the rain knowing that it will get me 1 percent closer to my goal. It doesn't have to be pretty. It doesn't have to be my fastest time. I just need to *do* it. I take a deep breath, grit my teeth, give myself a quick pep talk, and begin to run.

When I was formulating my twelve stones, the core tenants that I had observed in great leaders throughout my life, I knew I had to start with *grit*. Growing up in southern Louisiana, I can't think of a community that embodies grit more. No matter how many hurricanes have tried to knock us out, we know how to band together, put on our big boy and big girl pants, and buckle down as we clean up the debris to rebuild better and stronger. It is one of the things that makes me proud to be from Louisiana. We know how to overcome adversity without letting it destroy us. It's not always fun or easy, but we grit our teeth and go through the hardship, even though we know another hurricane will inevitably come. We don't let the future possibility of another storm deter us from living our best life. We get knocked down, we rebuild, we keep living, and we repeat. That is what great leaders do.

Stepping Stone: Grit Is Being Comfortable with the Uncomfortable

Great leaders are comfortable with adversity, hard times, and big changes. We've all heard the phrase that the only constant in life is change, but a lot of people are fearful of change. It makes them uncomfortable because there is an element of the unknown, the unexpected. Great leaders learn to become comfortable with the uncomfortable. They realize that life is filled with change whether they like it or not, so they might as well learn to handle it.

Sometimes change can be great, and other times it can be difficult, but it is always for a season. Those seasons will come and go, and new seasons will replace them. When the difficult seasons come, great leaders grit their teeth and lead their team through those times, knowing it will not permanently knock them down.

There have been times in my life when I went through bouts of deep depression, and just the thought of getting out of bed felt like a monumental task. Shortly after my divorce, I went through a pain cave of depression. I lost thirty pounds and my hair was falling out, but despite the physical symptoms, I'm not sure how many people knew I was truly depressed. Don't get me wrong, everyone handles depression differently.

For me, I was an incredibly high-functioning, over-performing depressive. It was how I had coped with a lot of trauma throughout my life. And this time, with three young kids, I felt like I had to cope this way again.

It was only because of God and my kids that I kept getting out of bed each morning when I wanted to wallow under the covers. For those people who know me, that is very uncharacteristic of me. I am naturally a positive, optimistic person. I have lived through a childhood of poverty and abuse. I have lived through Hurricane Katrina. But for some reason, going through a divorce was mentally and emotionally more difficult than all those other circumstances.

In addition to grieving the death of my marriage, my mother was also dying a slow and painful death from a long battle with breast cancer. I was doubly grieving. What I didn't realize until I started going to therapy was that I had been using business and busyness to keep me from dealing with a lot of issues that had been stuffed deep down. The divorce and caring for my dying mother as cancer ravaged not only her body but her brain and personality were the catalysts that forced me to deal with those wounds.

During that time, I had to clear away the debris of my own life and begin rebuilding, just like Louisianans do after a hurricane. And let me tell you, it was hard! I definitely developed a new level of grit during that time. I was working in real estate, homeschooling my three kids, and taking them with me to real estate classes and seminars at night and on weekends so that I could learn more about the industry and become a better Realtor. I can remember sitting in the backs of conference rooms while my kids did their homework and I took notes. I listened to Realtors who had gritted their way through other recessions and were sharing the lessons they learned to help us through the long-term aftermath of the 2008 financial crisis.

I was juggling a lot of responsibility as a mom, a homeschool teacher, a breadwinner, a businesswoman, and a daily fighter of a deep, two-year depression. I clung to routine, discipline, and faith to help me grit my way through.

I honestly don't know how people have grit without God. In the times when depression felt like an insurmountable pain cave that I would never get out of, I clung tightly to Jeremiah 29. Most people quote Jeremiah 29:11 which says, "'I know the plans I have for you'—this is the Lord's declaration—'plans for your welfare, not for disaster, to give you a future and a hope'" (HCSB). Now, I *love* this verse. It is such an encouraging verse, but so many people view it in a vacuum rather than reading the entire chapter to get its true context.

Jeremiah 29:1–10 talks about a seventy-year period of trials and tribulations that the Israelites, who were exiled from Jerusalem and forced to live in the pagan city of Babylon, were about to endure. God told the Israelites that their time in Babylon would be difficult: "The exile will be long. Build houses and settle down. Plant gardens and eat their produce" (v. 28 HCSB). God was saying, *Buckle up, buttercup; it's gonna get hard*, but he also gave them the promise of hope in Jeremiah 29:14, which encouraged them that if they would just grit their teeth and keep putting one foot in front of the other, they would see blessings: "'I will be found by you'—this is the Lord's declaration—'and I will restore your fortunes and gather you from all the nations and places where I banished you'—this is the Lord's declaration. 'I will restore you to the place I deported you from'" (HCSB).

Part of having or developing grit is knowing what your purpose is. I touched on this in chapter 1: "Great leaders know their 'why.'" Your why is your God-given purpose, the reason you were put here on this planet. Like we discussed in chapter 1, when you know your purpose, it helps you to find your assignment. If you know your why, your mission, you can feel confident showing up for whatever assignment the Lord has called you to, even when you don't feel like it. Success is not based on feelings or emotions. Grit is living your purpose and choosing to wake up every day wanting to make an impact, even if it's just having an impact on one person's life. I like to describe grit as asking *How can I make today 1 percent better than yesterday?* Just 1 percent. It may not sound like a lot, but when you're struggling and fighting through the day or a particular season with every ounce of grit you possess, that 1 percent becomes so meaningful. It is continued growth in a forward direction in pursuit of your purpose.

> Grit is living your purpose and choosing to wake up every day wanting to make an impact.

Stepping Stone: Grit Is Putting One Foot in Front of the Other When You Want to Quit

On the days when it's raining and I am soaked to the skin, my shoes heavy with water and rubbing blisters on my feet with each step, it can be tempting to give up running. It can be easy to quit and wonder why I am putting myself through this discomfort and pain. At those times, I remember what Winston Churchill told the British soldiers during World War II: "This is the lesson: never give in, never give in, never, never, never, never—in nothing, great or small, large or petty—never give in except to convictions of honour and good sense. Never yield to force; never yield to the apparently overwhelming might of the enemy."[18]

We have an enemy who is trying to prevent us from achieving our God-given purpose, our why. Jesus told us, "The thief does not come except to steal, and to kill, and to destroy. I have come that they may have life, and that they may have it more abundantly" (John 10:10 NKJV). The devil comes to rob you and tempt you to quit in the moments of discomfort and pain. I am here to encourage you not to let him! Keep putting one foot in front of the other. Another way to think of grit in this case is *perseverance*.

I love using ultrarunning analogies because, for me, the imagery is so clear. The only way forward is to literally keep putting one foot in front of the other. I'm currently training for my fifty-mile run, but when I lined up at the starting line for my forty-miler, it was easy to become overwhelmed by that distance. Yet when you run an ultra, there are aid stations that break the distance down into smaller, more manageable goals. Instead of letting myself become psyched out by the thought of completing forty miles without stopping, I focused on getting to that first aid station. I meditated on that first leg of the race. When I reached that first station, I focused on the next station. Usually, those first few aid stations are manageable in my own strength. Where things get difficult and you really have to persevere is when you must run through the dark.

It's easy to trust your own strength when the sun is out and you can see those aid stations in the distance. The path before you is lit and clear. But when the sun sets, it's a different story. I once did an ultra that started at midnight. Even though I had done several ultras before, when you are running through darkness, things get really trippy. Your senses begin to lie to you. You will start to hear and see things that aren't there. You hallucinate. Your brain will cause a noise that you rationally know is just a bird or an animal to feel like an imminent threat. Fear takes over. In those moments when you are running through the pitch-black woods with nothing but a little headlamp to light your path, you have no choice but to keep putting one foot in front of the other. If you stop, you're stuck! Not only will you be disqualified from the race, but you will be trapped out in the wilderness until someone can rescue you. You *have* to keep moving to reach the next aid station.

Your brain will start lying to you, telling you that you will never reach that aid station. When you hit that pain cave in darkness, things become exponentially worse. You have to fight your senses, you have to fight the physical pain and exhaustion from running for hours on end, and you have to fight the inner demons in your brain telling you to quit. It is easy for ultrarunners to stray off course during this time and feel even more lost. You can't even think about the finish line because it is all you can do to just keep moving. I cannot tell you how dark and painful these moments are for a runner, but when you persevere and keep putting one foot in front of the other, you will find your path again and see the sunrise.

Those sunrise moments make everything worthwhile. You forget about the pain cave and see the woods bathed in the most spectacular light. The clouds reflect a hundred different colors, and the warmth of the new sunrise brings life and warmth back into your bones. It clears the darkness that has hidden your path and plagued your mind, and you realize how silly you would have felt if you had given up. The aid station is suddenly visible again, and you realize how close you really were to it the whole time. Crossing the finish line feels manageable again. It won't be easy, you will still have to fight each step of the way through the exhaustion to get there, but you know you have a fighting shot. Like Churchill said, encouraging the British troops to keep fighting the seemingly invincible enemy in WWII, "Never give in!" Keep putting one foot in front of the other. Don't let the devil rob you of your finish line.

Stepping Stone: Grit Is Going to God for His Strength in Your Weakness

What sets female leaders apart, at least where grit is concerned, is the fact that women aren't afraid to ask for help. We find strength in community and prioritize doing life together. The deep relationships that women naturally build, even in the workplace, form a bond of sisterhood that women use to bolster each other when one is struggling. Again, this is not to say that men don't have bonds and teams, but women inherently gravitate to other women with more vulnerability and transparency. Men model strength and, in doing so, will often hide away their fears and insecurities so as not to undermine their position. They will shoulder burdens alone. Women do the opposite.

Women share things, create connections over common struggles, learn from each other's experiences, encourage each other, and empathize with each other. All of these things provide a support system and relational infrastructure when one's grit begins to waver.

Think about when you have a bad day. You have that one girlfriend you can always call who will reinvigorate you. Support is such a beautiful thing that women do for each other, and it's part of the way God designed women. As leaders, it is part of our role to do this for the women whom we are responsible for leading in our sphere of influence. But we also need to find women who can give us the tough love and remind us to put on our big girl pants, grit our teeth, and keep pursuing our God-given purpose in life and in business so that together we can finish our race strong.

However, what really sets great leaders apart is when they go to God for his strength in their weakness. Going back to the pain cave illustration with ultrarunning, there comes that point when every runner feels like the pain is too great, the depression is too great, the insurmountable obstacles they're facing are too great, and they are tempted to give up and quit. Everyone has that point when they think life will break them. Yet that's what keeps us on our knees going to God. Without that breakdown point, we wouldn't need God. We could do it in our own strength. It's when we reach our human breakdown point that God gives us his breakthrough point. God gives us supernatural grit.

> It's when we reach our human breakdown point that God gives us his breakthrough point. God gives us supernatural grit.

So many times I hear people misquote 1 Corinthians 10:13. They will mistakenly say that God won't give us more than we can handle, but that is not what that verse actually says. The verse says, "No temptation has overtaken you except such as is common to man; but God is faithful, who will not allow you to be tempted beyond what you are able, but with the temptation will also make the way of escape, that you may be able to bear it" (NKJV). God is telling us that we will face temptation, even very hard temptation that we cannot handle alone, but we will not be overcome by it. Even Jesus faced temptation in the desert in Matthew 4. Satan tempted Jesus when he was at his weakest. He had had no food, no water, and he was in the hot desert for forty days and forty nights. And you think ultrarunning is a test of endurance! It's nothing, really, compared to what Jesus faced in the desert. Plus, Satan knew exactly how to tempt Jesus, just as he studies each and every one of us to exploit our individual weaknesses. He targeted Jesus at the depth of his (human) pain cave.

We are so used to focusing on Jesus as sinless and perfect, and it can be hard to remember that he was tempted just like we are. He was fully flesh and blood. I'm betting that the offer to turn stones into bread looked pretty good after an epic desert fast! And how did Jesus combat the devil? Grit and God. He dug down deep into his training, his knowledge of Scripture. In the midst of that intense temptation and weakness, he cried out to his heavenly Father to give him strength. Grit and God got him through that pain cave and defeated the devil, but before that breakthrough moment when the angels came down and ministered to Jesus, rebuilding his strength and rewarding his perseverance, he had to go through a breaking point. How much more do we, as imperfect humans, need to rely on grit and God!

If you picture your God-given purpose—that thing that causes you to get out of bed, get dressed, and line up at the starting line; that mission that you and only you were put on this earth to achieve—and you grit your teeth to push through the breaking point in the pain cave, you will find your breakthrough.

Grit is an inner resolve, a character trait, that won't let you stay down, and it is one of the key traits I always look for when I am hiring someone for a position of leadership. When I am hiring someone, I want to know, "Will this person be able to keep showing up day after day when the dream job suddenly feels like a nightmare? Will they keep getting up each morning and putting on clothes when depression hits and they want to stay home because their emotions are screaming for them to call in sick?"

Grit is a muscle. And just like any other muscle, it's built by becoming comfortable with the uncomfortable and the difficult. We build our grit each day by getting up even when we want to stay in bed, by putting one foot in front of the other when we want to quit, and by going to God and asking him for his divine strength in our weakness. When we practice grit, we have the resilience to sweep away the debris, rebuild, and keep going when the storms and hurricanes of life come. It's a deliberate choice to keep moving onward and upward rather than succumb to excuses and victimization when you get knocked down.

> Grit is a muscle. And just like any other muscle, it's built by becoming comfortable with the uncomfortable and the difficult.

I'm not going to lie; it will be difficult. I fully believe that grit is embracing the hard. Grit doesn't mean ignoring the reality of the pain cave. It does mean acknowledging that the process will be difficult but grabbing onto it and doing it anyway. Grit isn't passive. Quitting is passive. Grit is active. You get better at it by practicing it daily. I want to encourage you to start building those muscles of grit today so that they are strong when you need them. God *will* allow you to go through more than you can handle on your own, but he will also be there to give you his strength to keep going.

4

Stone 2: Leaders Fail Forward

As leaders and as businesswomen, we strive for success. It is the goal. No matter what success may look like to each individual, we all have some mental picture of success that we are working toward. But what happens when we inevitably *fail*? Nobody teaches us how to deal with that terrifying four-letter word. It is as if society systemically trains us to believe that failure is somehow a reflection of our personhood. There is the detrimental misconception that if we fail at something, it is because we are failures at our core. That is not true, and it is such a damaging way to go through life. Not only does it negatively affect our self-esteem, but it also keeps us from taking risks because we fear failure.

Great leaders, however, fail forward. They let failure move them closer to success. This might seem like an oxymoron, but that's why I want to reframe and redefine the concept of failure for you because, let me tell you, everybody will fail at something at least once in their life. There is no escaping it.

I have failed so many times in my personal life, my professional life, my spiritual life, and my relational life. I guarantee you that if you asked every successful person you admire about the number of times they failed before they were successful, the failures would far outweigh the successes. Success is a snapshot of all the failures it took to become successful. It does not happen overnight. There is no shortcut to success. However, failure is not something that we need to be afraid of. It is not a reflection of who we are as people and as women at our core. Failure is just a tool we use to learn. Yes, some failures will feel bigger and more painful than others, but it is how we reframe failure, brush ourselves off, and learn from it that ultimately determines or limits our future success.

> Success is a snapshot of all the failures it took to become successful.

I see too many women feel the embarrassment of a failure so deeply that they decide to let that one momentary failure cap their future potential. Unfortunately, I believe that is partly due to how women are raised. Girls are not taught from a young age to brush themselves off after failing the same way that boys are.

Stepping Stone: Leaders Learn to Pick Themselves Up Again When They Fail

Think about how you parent your children or how you were parented as a child. A little boy falls off his bicycle, skins his knees, and begins to cry. Most parents are going to tell that little boy, "Hey, it's okay. You're tough. Brush the dirt off, get back on that bike, and keep trying!" We are teaching boys to be resilient and have grit—just like we discussed in the last chapter—and to handle failures as opportunities to learn not to repeat the same mistake.

But for little girls, the same scenario plays out a little differently. When a little girl falls off her bike, skins her knees, and begins to cry, momma rushes over to her and says, "Aw, baby, let's go inside and clean that up. Lemme kiss it, make it better. You need to be more careful next time. Put on knee pads."

All that extra fuss over the little girl teaches her that she is fragile. She is delicate. She needs to be more cautious or tentative or, dare we say, *fearful* of the outside world. The perception of fear we have surrounding failure puts an imagined lid on our potential that is exponentially lower than the true potential of our God-given abilities. We draw attention to the girl's pain and the scar rather than dusting her off like we do the little boy and immediately reinforcing that the boy is going to be okay and can keep playing despite the boo-boo. We also teach our daughters that scars are something to hide, even while teaching our sons that scars are cool and tough. Is it any wonder, then, that women grow up to be more risk-averse?

Now, of course, this is an overly simplified example that discounts the complex biological differences that also factor into decision-making. But you get the idea. As women, we have to do a better job of reframing failure for ourselves and reacting to failure as parents. Failure is not the end of the world. Failure is how we grow, evolve, and innovate. To fail is human.

Instead of letting the emotions and shock associated with failing prevent us from getting back up, get back up. In John Maxwell's book *Failing Forward*, he looked for commonalities among high-achieving people. Expecting to find contributing factors like access to wealth, stability, or opportunity that gave high achievers a head start in life, he discovered that none of these factors guaranteed success. What he did discover was that high achievers reframed failure in their minds. They didn't let it keep them down; rather, they immediately picked themselves back up and tried a new approach.[19]

I've heard that the first thing that horse riders learn when they get thrown to the ground is to get back on that horse. The longer you wait to climb back up, the harder it becomes. The fear has time to settle in, and the pain has time to take root. The same can be said of life. When we choose to pick ourselves up, dust ourselves off, and get right back up on that horse, we are teaching ourselves to be resilient. We will try to avoid the repetition of the pain and embarrassment of the same failure by adapting new strategies to improve the results of our efforts.

But here's another important distinction that I believe gets easily muddied: failure does not always equal sin. Yet we certainly treat it like some inherently fatal flaw that we must avoid at all costs and mentally beat ourselves up over. Sin is an issue of the heart usually stemming from an immoral desire. Failure is simply making a mistake or not meeting a goal, sometimes out of ignorance or by accident. Regardless, sin can be forgiven, and we can learn from failures because of Jesus. If we were perfect, we would have no need for a Savior. Where sin is concerned, Jesus saves us from our immoral souls. Where failure is concerned, Jesus can stand in the gap as the perfect rabbi or teacher.

> Where sin is concerned, Jesus saves us from our immoral souls. Where failure is concerned, Jesus can stand in the gap as the perfect rabbi or teacher.

In 2 Corinthians 12:9–10, Paul wrote, "He said to me, 'My grace is sufficient for you, for power is perfected in weakness.' Therefore, I will most gladly boast all the more about my weaknesses, so that Christ's power may reside in me. So I take pleasure in weaknesses, insults, catastrophes, persecutions, and in pressures, because of Christ. For when I am weak, then I am strong" (HCSB). That's a pretty extreme way to reframe failures!

I'll be honest, I don't know that I would want to go around boasting about and taking pleasure in some of the failures I've had. What I believe the Bible is trying to teach us here, though, is that we have the power to shift how we perceive our failures. Romans 5:3–5 gives us more rationale behind learning to reframe our failures: "We also rejoice in our afflictions, because we know that affliction produces endurance, endurance produces proven character, and proven character produces hope. This hope will not disappoint us, because God's love has been poured out in our hearts through the Holy Spirit who was given to us" (HCSB).

This verse should give us great comfort and courage to pick ourselves up when we fail because it shares that God uses the moments of affliction, wherever they stem from, to build resilience, build character, and even build hope. God tells us that he is not disappointed in us when we fail. He pours out his love for us through the Holy Spirit like a loving parent and tells us, *It's okay. You're okay. Now dust yourself off and keep going.*

Stepping Stone: Leaders View Failure as a Learning Experience

With Romans 5:3–5 in mind, I have learned to wake up every morning and pray, *Okay God, I'm ready to fail today. Help me to learn from it and protect me from my shortcomings.* This may seem extreme, but I have learned to trust God's promises and embrace failure because I know that James 1:2 says "Consider it a great joy, my brothers, whenever you experience various trials" (HCSB). I have learned to consider it a joy to have trials and failures because it teaches perseverance and, through perseverance, I have been able to discover success. I view each failure as an opportunity to learn.

I have gone through so many James 1:2 journeys. When I graduated college, I began working for a major pharmaceutical company as a sales representative. Remember, I grew up poor, living in a trailer and working three jobs to help support my family. I had never been on an airplane until my junior year of college. I was lucky if we went out to eat at a restaurant once a year. Yet here I was, twenty-two years old, responsible for traveling all around the country and entertaining medical doctors at fancy restaurants while teaching them about the pharmaceuticals I was selling. This was way before the days of Google and smart phones. I had a beeper and one of those prehistoric flip phones.

When I first sat down at a fancy restaurant and saw how many different forks, knives, and glasses were set in front of me on the table, I had *no idea* what to do. I was so embarrassed as I fumbled my way through the dinner trying not to have a panic attack. The next day the first thing I did was find a bookstore and buy Emily Post's *Etiquette in Society, in Business, in Politics, and at Home*. I read that book from cover to cover several times, making notes and teaching myself not to make the same faux pas the next time I entertained doctors. After a few months, I became comfortable with fine dining and traveling to the point where I began to relax and enjoy it.

I could have viewed my ignorance due to my impoverished backwoods upbringing as humiliating (and it was), but I didn't let it stop me. I picked myself up, brushed myself off, and got back on the bicycle. I had learned to fail forward.

When I decided to leave pharmaceutical sales so I could stay home and have a family, I decided to open up my own coffee shop called Mochaccinos. This was during the early days of Starbucks and the coffee craze. I had fallen in love with coffee while sitting at many tables with doctors around the country as a pharmaceutical representative. I loved the ritual associated with post-meal coffee, the way it brought people together after discussing business all throughout a meal, allowing them to relax and decompress. It allowed the protective walls to come down after the meal-time ritual of pitching and performing, and it finally gave people permission to be more transparent and authentic. Owning a coffee shop and making my love for this experience of bonding over a hot beverage into my primary business seemed like the perfect next step for me—only I didn't know the first thing about running a coffee shop.

I had been a pre-med student. I had spent my collegiate career poring over biology and anatomy books. I had never once taken a business class. I didn't even know what a business plan was. When I showed up to the bank to ask for a loan, I didn't even know how much I needed to ask for to start my business. I didn't know where to source coffee beans or espresso machines. The poor loan officer, God bless her, had to explain to me all the things I needed before she could even consider my request for a loan.

Again, I could have let the embarrassment and the overwhelming lack of knowledge kill my dream right then and there. Instead, I went to the library and checked out every book on running a coffee house I could find (again, these were pre-Google days!). I opened the yellow pages and called up every local coffee shop to ask who their suppliers were and if they would be interested in mentoring me. Even on the day I opened the coffee shop—our grand opening—I realized I hadn't hired a single employee to help take the orders, fix the coffee, or keep the books. I faced a line out the door from my wonderfully supportive (and patient) community while I fumbled around trying to do everything by myself.

Eventually, I'm happy to say, I got my "stuff" in order and got the hang of it. I eventually hired baristas; I hired a bookkeeper; I hired an accountant and payroll company; I built an infrastructure through much trial and error; and I eventually failed my way forward into franchising my coffee shop into seven successful locations across southeast Louisiana. However, I surprise a lot of people by saying that when I sold Mochaccinos after Hurricane Katrina in 2007, I consider it to be one of my biggest professional failures.

Most people would imagine that selling a franchise would be the pinnacle of success, but for me, it wasn't. I had grown too big, too fast, and as a homeschool mom of three kids with a husband pushing me into real estate, I no longer had the bandwidth or systems to sustain continued growth of my franchise. Even though the franchise had become successful enough to sell, I wasn't prepared to handle the growth and had stretched myself too thin. It wasn't the celebratory company buyout that most people would equate with success. Instead, it felt like a failure. I had sold out on a business I had birthed, grown, and loved. I didn't have the bandwidth, infrastructure, and resources to keep fostering it by myself.

Every now and again I wonder what it might have turned into had I taken a step back, dusted myself off, found new mentors, and kept riding that bicycle. However, God knew that I would never leave Mochaccinos if I wasn't pushed out of the proverbial boat that had become too safe and comfortable for me. He knew that real estate was where he could use me and that there would be plenty of new risks, failures, and successes to come with another major career change.

This is why, when I speak, I prioritize talking about failure and how great leaders fail forward. I think it is so important to reframe the concept of failing from a thing we fear, something that can paralyze us because we let it impact our identity, into an instrument of bettering ourselves. Unless we go through the learning curve of James 1:2, we cannot arrive into the achievement and promise that comes in James 1:4: "Endurance must do its complete work, so that you may be mature and complete, lacking nothing" (HCSB).

Too often, we look at someone who is successful and wish we could have come to success as easily. We are making an incorrect assumption based on a snapshot we are seeing. Their success is the highlight reel of the countless hours of struggle, failures, resilience, and perseverance that we didn't get to see. We didn't see the James 1:2 portion of their life.

Make no mistake, there is no easy path to becoming a successful leader, but we do not have to fear failure. We can reframe it as a learning tool. I firmly believe that God did not design failure to punish us or to dissuade us from taking risks. The Bible even says so! Failures can be wonderful opportunities that teach us to take a step back, assess the situation, find where we got off track, surround ourselves with wise counselors, and continue educating ourselves so we can move forward. It better equips us for the next level of success. As women, it is time to embrace failure and use it to bring us closer to God and closer to our goals. Thank God for the failures in your life and use them to develop resilience and perseverance so you can fail forward.

> We do not have to fear failure. We can reframe it as a learning tool.

5

Stone 3: Leaders Create Growth Plans

Do you need a coffee warm-up yet? Because we are about to set the scene for you to reach achievement. So go pop that coffee in the microwave and grab your thinking cap.

I am going to take you through an exercise I love to use when I speak. It is all about reflecting on your why and creating a growth plan, or action plan, to get there. Think of it as eating that proverbial elephant one bite at a time.

When I get to this stone, I love to ask an audience the following question: "What does your retirement look like?" I usually let this question sit for a few moments to give people time to think. Nobody ever likes to volunteer their answer first. Some even look confused as if they've never pondered this question. There will inevitably be that one jokester who says, "Retirement? Dawn, I can barely afford today!"

Then the room begins to relax a little, setting up my second question: "How many of your parents had a retirement plan?" Most people will raise their hands.

"Let me guess," I venture. "How many of your parents' retirement plans looked like buying an RV and traveling the country?" Again, most hands go up.

"How many of your parents actually bought their RV?"

A lot of hands go down. Only a few people will still have their hands raised.

I ask, "Did that RV ever leave the driveway and, if it did, were your parents in good enough health to enjoy the retirement they dreamed of?"

The remaining hands go down, and a heavy wake-up call settles over the room.

According to a Harvard Medical School study, the average life expectancy of the American male is about seventy-three years and the average life expectancy of the American female is about seventy-nine years.[20] Meanwhile, the average retirement age is sixty-five years for American men and sixty-two years for American women, according to a 2021 study by the Center for Retirement Research at Boston College.[21] If you do the quick math, the average American is anticipating at least a decade in which they should not have to work full-time and can enjoy the fruits of retirement.

But the reality is that most Gen X and aging millennial Americans are not only financially unprepared for their future retirement, but they also have no idea what they want their retirement to look like. This is where growth plans are necessary. A growth plan starts with the end in mind and helps create a practical action plan for you to reach those goals. But first, you need to have what I am going to call those "life goals."

> A growth plan starts with the end in mind and helps create a practical action plan for you to reach those goals.

Let's go back to the question of your why, that reason God put you on this earth. That is your *mission*. Before you can begin working on your growth plan, you have to know your why. I discovered my why back in 2012 during a sabbatical I took to get away with God for a weekend of prayer and fasting. I was struggling with a failing marriage, raising three young children, and caring for my mom who was dying of breast cancer.

My dad had died when I was in high school, so I never got to see either of my parents enjoy a retirement. All these things were weighing on my mind, and I cried out to God wondering what I was here for. What I was working for. And as God often does in that still, silent voice, he gave me my why.

Dawn, he said, *I have called you to an abundant life. I want you to impact the lives of others by being the hands and feet of Christ so they, too, can experience the abundant life.*

That revelation completely changed my life. It gave me my life goal. My purpose. I knew what I was here to do and what I was ultimately working toward. How many times have we heard the Scripture paraphrased that God is no respecter of persons? I love the way the Holman Christian Standard Bible translates this verse: "Now I really understand that God doesn't show favoritism" (Acts 10:34 HCSB). That means that if God can reveal my purpose, my why, to me, he can do it for you too. My why was to be one of servant leadership, which is another reason I am writing this book. I want to help women discover their whys and give them the tools to achieve their goals. That brings me back to our growth plan. Let's create one together. Grab your coffee and a pen and notebook.

Stepping Stone: Start with the End in Mind

I have observed that great leaders have growth plans which keep them focused toward their life goals so they can overcome life's unexpected obstacles when the roadblocks arise or moments of distraction get them off track. The growth plan is like the road map that helps you figure out how to get back on course and finish strong. It provides an outline of what you need to manifest your mission.

In the Old Testament, God instructed Habakkuk, "Write down this vision; clearly inscribe it on tablets so one may easily read it" (Habakkuk 2:2 HCSB). Writing down the vision helps keep it at the forefront of your mind. I want you to write down your life goal. Is it to travel more? Get in better shape so you can be healthy enough to spend time with your grandkids? You have to know what you're working toward so you can lay the stepping stones to get you there.

My husband, Manly, and I want to travel more, and we want to continue investing in real estate. We have the dream of building a retreat center where people can come and have sabbaticals and getaways where they can be refreshed. That is our retirement goal as a couple. But I also have personal goals. I want to run a hundred-mile ultramarathon. I want to continue writing books and speaking to women and being that servant leader of God.

So together, Manly and I have our master growth plan. This is our combined plan for our retirement, which we then have broken down into a ten-year plan, a five-year plan, and a one-year plan. We then have our individual ten-, five-, and one-year growth plans, and we make those for every area of our lives that we want to grow in. Remember, leaders never stop growing. So for every area in which you have a life goal, you need a growth plan to keep you moving onward and upward.

When I set my fitness goal to run a hundred-mile ultramarathon, I created a growth plan. I first started with running 10Ks, then marathons, then ultramarathons. I hired coaches to train me. (I am a big believer in having coaches to help you reach your goals, which I will discuss in greater detail in chapter 7.) I knew that I would need people smarter than me on my team, people who had already achieved the goals I was setting, people who had failed forward and could help me avoid the same mistakes on my way to meeting my running goals.

I worked with my coaches to set up nutrition programs; fitness programs for running, strength, and endurance training; and mental toughness programs to get me through those pain caves. As I write this book, I am coming up on the end of my five-year ultrarunning plan to run a fifty-miler for my fiftieth birthday. It has been five years of training for this big milestone and completing thirty-mile and forty-mile races. My fitness growth plans set benchmarks to help me build on each year's successes to reach those larger milestones.

Stepping Stone: Create a Growth Plan for Every Area You Want to Grow

In addition to my fitness growth plan, I also have growth plans for my marriage, my finances, my spiritual life, and my professional goals. Manly and I make a habit of going away together several times every year for a sabbatical to reflect on the past year and plan for the future year. As a couple and as individuals, we look at how we met our goals for the previous year. What did we accomplish? What didn't we accomplish? Where did we get off track? What did we say yes to that maybe we should have said no to? Because time is one of our most precious commodities, something in which we are limited to for a finite period, I believe it is our God-given responsibility to steward it as wisely as possible. One way in which Manly and I have learned to become better stewards of our time is through sabbaticals. Sabbaticals (which we will discuss further in chapter 15) are a time of reflection—of getting alone with God and with each other—that allows us to evaluate first what got us closer to our goals in the past year and second what we need to do differently in the year to come to keep us on track for our short-term and long-term goals. Manly and I have discovered that the fourth quarter is the best time for us to do our growth plan evaluations because it is usually a slower time of year for us work-wise. For a long time, the real estate market would calm down in the month of December, allowing us to get away for a few days. Times have changed in the last few years and it's not quite as calm as it used to be, but we still make a point to take time for a fourth-quarter sabbatical. Sometimes we have to say "no" to other social things and be intentional about taking a day away from the holiday craziness to do our sabbatical, but it is always worth the sacrifice because of what it means to our future goals.

While Manly and I put special significance on our fourth-quarter sabbatical as a way to set the new year up for success, we also try to sit down together quarterly to review and adjust our yearly growth plans. We know that unexpected things have a way of popping up throughout the year and, rather than letting the whole year go by before we readjust, we like to amend our growth plans every few months so that we don't get too far off track. Make no mistake, there is discipline and sacrifice involved in making, amending, and keeping growth plans but we know the short-term sacrifice is worth the long-term gain. In that way, it's like my mornings: I don't want to get up every single morning at 4:44 a.m. to run, yet I know the investment in my future is worth the time, effort, and extra hour of sleep.

I am a firm believer that for every area where you want to grow or where you have a goal, you should create a growth plan. Want a better marriage? Create a marriage growth plan and schedule regular dates. Want a better relationship with your kids? Create a family growth plan and schedule meaningful time doing things that will bring you closer together. Want to hear God better? Create a spiritual growth plan and schedule that prayer time. Want to see your finances in better shape? Create a financial growth plan to pay down your debt and find opportunities for investments and passive income. Want to see your business grow? Create professional growth plans to set KPIs, generate new leads, make more sales calls, and schedule the deadlines to meet them. Want to lose twenty pounds? Create a fitness growth plan and find a trainer or a class, look at your nutrition, and schedule that gym time. Want to run a marathon or an ultramarathon? Do I need to say it again? *Create that growth plan!* When we create growth plans, we can hit the ground running (no pun intended) come January 1 (or whenever we're starting to work toward a goal).

Especially as a leader, you have to work on yourself so you can be a more effective captain for your team. You model leadership to the people under you. If you want your team to continue growing, you have to lead by example. Start with the end in mind and use those growth plans to get you and your team 1 percent closer to meeting your goals every single day.

Stepping Stone: Your Goals Should Grow with You

When I started running, I didn't begin wanting to run ultramarathons. I could never have dreamed of running one hundred miles when I bought my first pair of running shoes. My first major running goal was to do a half-marathon. A half-marathon seemed like an extreme goal back then, but you know what happened? As I grew stronger and completed my first half-marathon, suddenly a marathon didn't seem so crazy. When I completed my first marathon, ultramarathons began to look more attainable. As I trained and developed endurance, I was able to set bigger goals. Your goals should also grow with you.

> As I trained and developed endurance, I was able to set bigger goals. Your goals should also grow with you.

When you reach a goal, sure, you could stop and be happy with what you've achieved, but great leaders are always learning, always growing. If you're young, you have an even greater opportunity to push yourself to see what is possible. When I create my short-term and long-term growth plans, I like to set goals that feel slightly out of reach. Even if I don't necessarily reach them by the original deadline that I set, I know that I got further than I would have if I'd aimed for what was merely comfortable.

One of my favorite Scripture passages is Philippians 3:13–14: "I do not consider myself to have taken hold of it. But one thing I do: Forgetting what is behind and reaching forward to what is ahead, I pursue as my goal the prize promised by God's heavenly call in Christ Jesus" (HCSB). This verse reminds me that as long as I am alive and have breath, I can keep striving for new goals.

I also love the prayer of Jabez in 1 Chronicles 4:10, which says, "Jabez called out to the God of Israel: 'If only You would bless me, extend my border, let Your hand be with me, and keep me from harm, so that I will not cause any pain.' And God granted his request" (HCSB). Jabez could have become comfortable with what he had achieved and settled. Instead, he prayed for God to continually enlarge his territory. God blesses that kind of mentality. That's the kind of mindset that shatters glass ceilings. I love when Manly and I sit down, look back on what we have been able to accomplish, and can dream bigger than we ever thought possible.

Growing up in the trailer park, I could not have imagined that I would be the regional director of the biggest and highest-performing division of a major international realty group. My dad dropped out of school in eighth grade to work and support himself at the age of thirteen. My mom stayed in school until she got pregnant with me in eleventh grade and had to drop out. To me, going to college was an extreme goal. With my father on disability from his accident, unable to work a steady job, the burden of financial responsibility fell on my mom and me. My first big goal was to graduate high school because neither of my parents had done that. Higher education was a luxury we couldn't afford. If I was going to make my college dream a reality, I knew I would have to get a scholarship, so that became what I intentionally worked toward. Even though I wasn't aware of what growth plans were when I was in high school, I had them. Every year, I set out to make the highest GPA in my class. I knew that I could potentially earn a scholarship if I kept my GPA high enough. Thankfully, the hard work paid off. When I found out I was awarded a scholarship to cover my tuition, I was ecstatic that I could achieve my dream of going to college.

I could have stopped there. I could have been happy knowing that I had completed the goal of getting into college and being the first person in my family to make it that far, but I chose to dream bigger. My dream expanded to not only go to college but also to graduate. As graduation got closer, I began to dream of the possibility of going to medical school.

That never would have seemed possible in high school, but successes compound and build confidence. In my last two years of college, I made med school the goal. Unfortunately, I didn't get a good enough score on my MCAT exam to get accepted into medical school on my first try, so I became a pharmaceutical rep so that I could save money while waiting until the following year to retake the exam. However, as I worked in pharmaceutical sales, I realized that going into medicine was not where my passion was.

Goals can change. Passions can change. Life can take you in new directions. Your growth plans should not be so ironclad that they prevent you from moving into different areas God might have for you. If I had been so dead set on going to med school, I would not be here writing this book. I probably would have made myself miserable and stressed trying to stay in a lane that wasn't the lane God meant for me.

By this time in my life, I was seeking God's will and open to his moving. When he placed the dream into my heart to open my own business, that excited me. I didn't have any experience or education in business, but as I described earlier, I learned how to create a business plan and opened my first Mochaccinos. Again, I could have been happy with that and enjoyed having opened a successful business, but I wanted God to enlarge my territory. Literally! I had seven Mochaccinos franchises when I sold the business. I could never have imagined that when I began.

When God led me into real estate, I continued to let my dreams grow with my successes. Whenever I met a goal, I would expand my goals for the next year and create new growth plans to help me get there. Today, I look back on my life and am blown away by what God has allowed me to do. It all started with a dream, a life goal to work toward. Even if that initial life goal does not end up being your ultimate goal, growth plans will help you accomplish the goals you set in life.

I am so glad I didn't stop at any of the original goals I had set for myself. I am so glad that I listened to God redirecting my path into new areas and invited him into the planning process. He has taken me further than I ever thought possible.

I encourage you to sit down and start dreaming. Think about where you want to end up and begin writing the plan. Invite God to help you create the stepping stones to get you there and then be willing to scale your vision and let your goals grow with you.

> Sit down and start dreaming. Think about where you want to end up and begin writing the plan.

6

Stone 4: Leaders Practice Discipline

Let's talk about discipline. In all the great leaders I have observed, regardless of their field, a consistent trait they all possess and practice is discipline. However, discipline is one of those words that most people initially (and sometimes viscerally) recoil at. They equate it with pain and intense discomfort. And they're not necessarily wrong. Look at Olympic athletes who put in countless hours at the gym, day in and day out, with the hopes of bringing home a medal. Don't you think there are days when they would rather sleep in or call in sick? Of course! Yet they know that if they are to compete at their best and have a chance to medal, the potential reward is worth the present cost.

Discipline is what makes those growth plans we discussed in the last chapter achievable. It's easy to confuse grit, which we discussed in chapter 3, with discipline; however, discipline is a long-term lifestyle choice. Grit is more of the "will call" version of discipline. A lot of people have grit but don't have discipline. Grit is an action; discipline is a habit. Grit is what you call on to get you through the pain cave you are facing in the present moment. Discipline is an established routine born out of conscious decision and sacrifices that are made day in and day out. Grit can be applied to get you through a tough situation in one area of life for a short burst. Highly disciplined people, on the other hand, have developed discipline in multiple areas of life for the long haul. Grit is like an espresso shot to give you a sudden energy boost whereas discipline is like putting premium gasoline in your car to sustain going the distance without damaging your engine.

> Grit is an action; discipline is a habit.

In this chapter, I want to completely reframe the way you think about discipline. Contrary to popular belief, discipline is not a dirty word. Discipline is what gets you past the emotional high of setting growth plans and keeps you going when obstacles arise. I believe that discipline is listening to logic instead of emotions.

Too many people, especially women, let their emotions dominate their decision-making. Emotions can lie to us. They can change on a whim. If you want to be a strong, effective, trustworthy leader, you cannot be guided by whims. You must listen to logic and be steadfast to help your team stay on course when things get difficult, and things *will* get difficult.

Where people attach a negative connotation to discipline, though, is in the self-sacrifice and rigidity of routine. People tend to have an extreme perception of what discipline looks like. There's a certain motivational guru who has written many books on discipline that I have followed and read for years. This guru was someone I looked up to because the discipline this individual practiced was so extreme, intense, and inspiring. But when I tried to implement this person's techniques, I continuously found myself failing. It was too much for where I was in my life and for the calling I had on my life.

That's when I realized that there is such a thing as healthy discipline and unhealthy discipline, and what might be healthy for one person could be unhealthy for another. You have to find the type of discipline that works for you. Going back to those Olympic athletes, we see discipline glorified in the extreme when, in reality, the average person does not need extreme-sized discipline. We need everyday-sized discipline.

I like to think of discipline as a methodology, a series of practical steps honed through trial and error that equip you with a tool kit you can dig through to keep you moving forward when obstacles come. I'm going to give you some stepping stones to help you reframe discipline as a positive methodology rather than a negative or intimidating one. I have learned to reframe discipline in my own life by discovering the difference between healthy and unhealthy discipline, using mind shifts instead of mind hacks, keeping my emotions between the lines, and utilizing what I call intentional guided discipline. All these different framing devices have helped me build a tool kit filled with a variety of tools to provide discipline when I need it, and it can do the same for you.

Stepping Stone: Leaders Know the Difference Between Healthy and Unhealthy Discipline

Did you have to revise some unhealthy habits you made during the COVID-19 lockdown? I know I did. It was so easy to fall into the practice of eating comfort food, binge-watching television until all hours of the night, and even enjoying an alcoholic beverage…or two…or three. Let's be real and transparent here. We would get on Zoom with our friends at 5 p.m. so that we weren't drinking alone and we would converse late into the evening. It became communal, connecting us in our isolation, and it became something we looked forward to. It was a way to soothe ourselves in a world that was suddenly scary, and it became a socially acceptable way of dealing with that fear and loneliness. But after lockdown ended, many of us kept those new habits going and found them hard to walk back.

It was difficult to start waking up at 4:44 a.m. again for a run, to turn the TV off and go to bed at a reasonable hour, to only have a glass of wine one night a week and not eat an entire pint of ice cream in one sitting.

But I knew that I had to break the unhealthy habits I had become disciplined in and re-form the healthy habits that I'd been disciplined in for much longer. I knew those healthy habits were responsible for keeping me moving toward the goals I wanted to reach long-term.

I also know myself well enough to know that I function best with structure and routine. It makes me feel secure, and I can sense a difference in my mental, emotional, and physical well-being when I am sticking to my routine as opposed to when I break it. It's the way I am wired as an individual, but I'll be the first to admit that at first it did not feel great to re-form those healthy habits. I had grown to like "the new normal." It felt good. It was complacent, and our brains are designed to crave comfort and complacency. But complacency leads to stagnation, and stagnation is the opposite of growth.

Even the Bible emphasizes the importance of discipline: "Now everyone who competes exercises self-control in everything. However, they do it to receive a crown that will fade away, but we a crown that will never fade away. Therefore I do not run like one who runs aimlessly or box like one beating the air. Instead, I discipline my body and bring it under strict control, so that after preaching to others, I myself will not be disqualified" (1 Corinthians 9:25–27 HCSB). Self-control and discipline go hand in hand because you have to practice dying to both self and what feels good in order to become stronger in discipline.

God knows that discipline doesn't feel good but that *we* will feel good when we practice it. God knows that humans are fickle and led by emotions. He knows that our emotions deceive us to give in to short-sighted temptations. I'm not even talking about harmful temptations. I'm talking about sleeping in instead of getting up to go to the gym, scrolling the phone during the hour you had set aside to work on the book you've been wanting to write for years, or eating out again after intending to cut back on that spending so that you could save extra money for a down payment on an income property. These are all examples of healthy discipline.

Healthy discipline still requires a short-term sacrifice on our part, but they are manageable sacrifices we can stick to. They are not unrealistic goals, which cause so many people to give up on the latest fad diets or overly strict, self-imposed New Year's resolutions. These require discipline beyond our skillset or need, and when we get frustrated, we give up. This is another reason why mind hacks (which we will discuss in a moment) do not work long-term. Our brains learn to outsmart those mind hacks in its search for what is easy to maintain.

If discipline were easy, we would all be great at it. Discipline is designed to have a degree of difficulty, but embracing healthy discipline helps you find that sweet spot where the difficulty becomes something you are willing to grit your way through because of the reward you are working toward. And as with any muscle that you exercise, the more you practice discipline, the easier it will become and the greater degree of discipline you will be able to sustain.

Stepping Stone: Leaders Keep Their Emotions Between the Lines

At Keller Williams, we have a saying: "Keep your emotions between the lines." I know I introduced this concept in chapter 2, but I want to discuss it further partly because I think it is so important, especially for women, and also because there's an element of discipline attached to steering our emotions.

Think about the lines on the road when you drive. You keep your car safely between those lines, knowing that if you drift outside of those boundaries, you could end up in a ditch or hit an oncoming car and cause a crash. The lines keep you moving forward safely. That's how great leaders handle emotions. They know that if they let their emotions drive, they will get off course. So they learn to keep their emotions in that safe zone between the lines. Again, this is especially important for women because we are naturally more emotional, empathetic, nurturing, and, let's be honest, hormonal than men. However, even though there are genetic factors in play where emotions are concerned, we can still develop the self-control and discipline needed to prevent those emotions from derailing us.

At the office, I have disciplined myself to be optimistic even when presenting difficult things to my team. I know that as a leader, I set the tone for my team. If I approach a situation negatively, it will trickle down and negatively affect my team's performance. I do not sugar coat or whitewash difficult things with my team. I present them with real data regarding obstacles in the market, but I choose to frame it in the context of "We will get through this together." I tell them I will have their backs during the difficult season, and I remind them that every tough season eventually passes and a new season begins. This casts a positive vision that, in turn, keeps them optimistic for the future. Keeping emotions between the lines helps you overcome the emotional highs and lows of life and lean into the grit we discussed in chapter 3. Great leaders know how and when to control their emotions.

This doesn't mean that I don't face fear during difficult seasons or go through periods when I doubt myself, my qualifications, and my leadership ability. I struggle with emotions just like the next gal. Sometimes it feels like a difficult season just *will not end*, and I am tempted to throw in the towel. But I have developed the mental discipline to shift my processing away from emotions and hold on to faith and logic. I have learned to keep my emotions between the lines, especially at work. I don't let my team see that uncertain side of me because I want to keep them moving onward and upward. I want them to trust me to lead them.

Sure, there are times for transparency with your team, but when the stuff hits the fan and they are looking to you to guide them, that is not the time or place for your cracks to be showing. You want to provide a calm demeanor and reassure those under your leadership that they will be okay—even if your emotions don't necessarily agree at that moment.

I have developed the discipline to save my emotional moments of doubt for my personal prayer time with God or one-on-one conversations with my husband. I let them love me through my emotional insecurities so I can show up to work strong, steady, and ready to lead. You have to transform your mental state and bring your actions in line with truth rather than emotion. Like the Bible tells us, "Do not be conformed to this age, but be transformed by the renewing of your mind, so that you may discern what is the good, pleasing, and perfect will of God" (Romans 12:2 HCSB). I like to think of transforming the mind as the discipline of practicing mind shifts. You have to look for the mind shift instead of the mind hack.

Stepping Stone: Leaders Use Mind Shifts Instead of Mind Hacks

Mind hacks are what I think of as single-use "quick fixes." All the mind hacks and life hacks we see on TikTok are not discipline; they are shortcuts. A popular mind hack I know I and many pro athletes use before competition is putting on a playlist to pump them up. How many times have we watched athletes arrive with big headphones on to help them get in the zone to perform? They've put in the training and the real discipline off the field, but they need that extra in-the-moment motivation to focus themselves and get their emotions and adrenaline pumping.

Another example of a mind hack is using mind games and mental math to trick our brains into doing something we would ordinarily put off. Who can relate to setting multiple alarms or setting their watch a little slow (when watches used to be analog) so you wouldn't be late somewhere? Or doing the calculations of nonessential tasks you can put off in the morning to give yourself a few extra minutes of sleep? Mind hacks are shortcuts we use to outsmart ourselves, positively or negatively, in order to perform better or justify procrastination to the point where we still are ultimately productive in the eleventh hour. They work in the moment, but they're not long-term solutions. Remember, there are no shortcuts to success.

Mind *shifts*, on the other hand, provide the grounds for long-term discipline because they literally shift the way your brain thinks. Mind hacks may work in the short-term when emotions are high and you're excited about discovering something that makes life seem easier, but we've already established that emotions are not trustworthy. When those emotions wear off, your brain will either figure out how to cheat its way around that mind hack or look for a different mind hack to get excited about. Mind shifts shift your perspective and general outlook on life. They shift the way you view and look at something. There's a saying that goes, "Change the way you look at things and the things you look at will change." You can't always control your first thought in response to something, but you *can* control your second thought. Mind shifts focus on challenging our thought patterns and our thought life, which in turn influences our actions.

> You can't always control your first thought in response to something, but you *can* control your second thought.

The Bible never talks about mind hacks, but it definitely talks about mind shifts. Romans 8:6 says, "The mind-set of the flesh is death, but the mind-set of the Spirit is life and peace" (HCSB). Here, the Bible tells us that the mindset of the flesh will not only derail us, but it can kill us. And we know from John 10:10 that "the thief does not come except to steal, and to kill, and to destroy. I have come that they may have life, and that they may have it more abundantly" (NKJV).

Discipline is a God-ordained tool that he knew we humans would need to control our emotionally driven flesh. The devil can often distract us from achieving God's why for our lives by keeping us focused on things that bring instant gratification to our flesh but are not serving us long-term. But when you know your why, discipline becomes a tool that

God gives us to help us resist the devil's shortsighted tricks so we can avoid giving into the temptations that get us off track.

God knew we would face temptation and weaknesses, and he presented us with a mind shift to bring our thoughts and actions up higher. Deuteronomy 6:6 tells us, "These words that I am giving you today are to be in your heart. Repeat them to your children. Talk about them when you sit in your house and when you walk along the road, when you lie down and when you get up. Bind them as a sign on your hand and let them be a symbol on your forehead. Write them on the doorposts of your house and on your gates" (HSCB). In other words, discipline provides the structure and routine that brings peace and order to our lives, and it is the mental toughness that influences our actions to come in line with God's greater plan for us moving forward.

Some of the people with the greatest discipline are recovering addicts and alcoholics. For those of you who know people who have gone through Alcoholics Anonymous (AA) or Narcotics Anonymous (NA), you are probably familiar with the regimented twelve-step program that they practice. For those of you who may not be familiar with a twelve-step program, it is a series of actions the recovering person must take to create a mind shift in their life. It gives them things to think about so they can break old destructive habits and form new healthy habits. It creates mental discipline that then translates into actionable discipline.

The twelve steps come from a place of humility and dependency on God or a "higher power," knowing that the human flesh is weak in the face of temptation. It encourages constant moral inventory-taking, which means practicing self-awareness of one's weaknesses.[22] And then the program institutes routine and order to make it easier for those in recovery to say no to the vices they know they are prone to.

Most people in recovery learn to stick to a strict schedule of waking up and going to sleep at the same time. They make their bed every day because it creates an atmosphere of cleanliness and order. They change their friendship circles and avoid the places they used to frequent where they would overindulge. Sobriety becomes such a singular goal for them that they shift their mental and physical habits to build the muscles of discipline so that they do not fall back into bad habits as easily.

But it takes work and sacrifice. Any alcoholic will tell you they are one drink away from falling off the wagon. They know how high the stakes are and what is at risk, but they also have mentors and accountability partners to help them stay the course. Everyone in recovery has a mentor who has battled with alcoholism or other addictions and leads by experience and example.

This structure always resonated with me because the Bible says, "Not many should become teachers, my brothers, knowing that we will receive a stricter judgment, for we all stumble in many ways. If anyone does not stumble in what he says, he is a mature man who is also able to control his whole body" (James 3:1–2 HCSB).

While this translation from James 3 uses the word *teachers*, in a historical context, the rabbis, or teachers, were the leaders of the church. Today the word *teachers* absolutely extends to anyone in leadership. And as leaders in any sphere of influence, we are called to higher purposes and higher standards because we have people following our example. We are not only responsible for our own performance but for theirs as well. It becomes even more important that we model discipline to our teams, but we cannot model what we do not practice ourselves. James warns us that leaders are prone to close scrutiny, and discipline is what prevents us from stumbling, but it first begins with the mind shift.

Stepping Stone: Leaders Practice Intentional Guided Discipline

Another way I like to practice healthy discipline is by utilizing intentional guided discipline. Intentional guided discipline builds on what we've already discussed about keeping emotions between the lines and developing sustainable mind shifts. But now we really take it to the next level. Now we become intentional and deliberate.

Some people confuse *intention* with *willpower*, but willpower, like emotions, is fleeting. It fluctuates based on how we feel. The intention comes with that mental shift wherein you are deliberately changing the way you think and bringing your actions in line with your thoughts. However, most people still can't do this on their own. That's where the guided part comes in. Most of us need someone to guide us and hold us accountable in our discipline.

I've always been a highly disciplined person. I had to be. I was helping my mom support my younger brother and sister from the time I was ten years old. I was working three jobs all through high school and college to make ends meet. My discipline muscles were already very strong. I can remember wanting so badly to use the money I had earned from working to buy a faux leather purse when I was about thirteen or fourteen. But discipline reminded me that my family needed it more.

It was hard giving every bit of money that I earned to my mom and not being able to spend any of it on little things I wanted. It was sacrifice, but I knew that sacrifice was for our family's greater good. We needed a roof over our heads, we needed to eat, we needed electricity, we needed shoes to go to school. So even though my childhood growing up in the trailer park may not have been idyllic, it instilled in me a work ethic and a discipline that was way beyond my years and has stuck with me.

For a long time, I was able to manage my discipline on my own until my growth plans and life goals got too big for me to do it on my own. I needed someone to guide me and instill new mind shifts to get me to that next level of discipline. As a result, I am a huge believer in coaching. Coaches can help you stick to your plans, but they can also guide you in what is most healthy and helpful for you in the moment.

Here's an example: While training for my fifty-mile ultramarathon, I was scheduled to run ten miles one Saturday morning. But because I had gone out to dinner and splurged with some friends the night before, I woke up at 4:44 feeling sluggish. Having conditioned myself to not listen to my emotions, I fully intended to push through the sluggishness, telling myself that I would feel proud of my accomplishment afterward. I already knew it wasn't going to be my best run, but I was aiming for just 1 percent better than the day before.

However, when I got into my run, my body began to cramp, and I began to feel pain. I had a decision to make—should I push through the pain and hope it would get better, or should I listen to my body, knowing that I had not fed it properly the day before? Had I been left to my own devices, I would have pushed through and probably hurt myself. Instead, I called my running coach.

I told my coach what was going on, and she immediately said, "Dawn, I want you to stop running right now and listen to your body. Your body is telling you that it needs rest, it needs good fuel, and it needs fluids. If you push through feeling the way you do right now, it will set you back." At that moment, I was so grateful for the guidance of my coach. She gave me intentional guided discipline that pivoted my plan, and she handed me the practical tools to get me back on track.

Sometimes we need someone on the outside to tell us that what we think is healthy discipline is turning into unhealthy discipline given particular circumstances. We need someone who has been where we want to go and who can redirect our plans, keeping the life goal in mind, and can also objectively remove emotion and feeling from the equation. My coach was able to be that objective sounding board who then offered intentional guidance using her experience and knowledge.

Intentional guided discipline is such a crucial yet underused tool that really separates good leaders from great leaders. Intentional guided discipline helps put tools in your tool kit that you can sort through and apply according to each day's individual challenges.

Stepping Stone: Leaders Build Their Discipline Kit

In ultrarunning, we carry a backpack that is known as our kit. My kit contains fluids, energy packets, food, flashlight, Band-Aids—a variety of tools that will keep me strong while I run. Depending on what I need at a given mile marker on my run, I can dig into my kit and pull out the tool that will help me keep running at that moment. I know that at different mile markers, I will need different tools.

> Discipline is not always one-size-fits-all.

In the same way, discipline is not always one-size-fits-all. I need different tools in my discipline kit at work than when I'm running or when I'm struggling with family and personal issues. Here are some of the discipline tools I keep at the ready in my kit.

- **Put On Real Clothes.** When I went through my period of depression, part of my discipline was getting out of bed every morning and putting on real clothes. Some days that was a monumental task because my emotions were screaming at me to stay in pajamas. But I knew that I would feel better mentally by engaging in that seemingly small act of self-care. It would make me look better, boost my confidence and self-esteem, and improve my mental well-being. Putting on real clothes was a tool in my kit that became part of my routine during that period of my life.

- **Use Guided Motivation.** Another discipline tool that has served me well is guided motivation. This is another tool I learned through ultrarunning. Guided motivation is when runners run the course in their mind before the race. They mentally visualize the course, and they envision themselves running it mile by mile. They visualize the pain cave, and they talk themselves through it. This way, when they actually reach the pain cave, they can use that mind shift to keep their emotions between the lines and grit their way through when their bodies are telling them to quit. They have disciplined their minds and bodies enough to keep moving forward toward the finish line they have already seen themselves crossing in their minds.

- **Collect Memorial Stones.** One of my favorite discipline tools is using memorial stones to celebrate the victories. We've already talked about how God instructed the Israelites in Joshua 4 to build memorial stones to remind themselves and future generations how God delivered them from their captors and provided for them in the wilderness. The memorial stones reminded them of the small victories on the way to the promised land because God knew how discouraged the Israelites would become while they wandered for forty years. The memorial stones are what inspired my 12 Stones Coaching, Speaking, and Consulting company. They are the moments that I have memorialized in my personal and professional life and want to hold on to when I am going through a difficult season.

- **Memorize Scripture.** I believe in memorizing Bible verses as part of my discipline kit. Psalm 37:31 says, "The instruction of his God is in his heart; his steps do not falter" (HCSB). The Bible also says, "This book of instruction must not depart from your mouth; you are to recite it day and night so that you may carefully observe everything written in it. For then you will prosper and succeed in whatever you do" (Joshua 1:8 HCSB). God knew how powerful a tool memorizing Scripture would be in keeping us on track with our growth plans. Scripture is what Jesus quoted when he was tempted by the devil. Clearly, he used the discipline of memorizing God's Word to resist temptation and keep from sin. Similarly, memorizing Scripture is part of our spiritual armor. It is our "sword of the Spirit," which, when we memorize it, is at the ready when temptation pokes at our weaknesses (Ephesians 6:10–18).

- **Ask, "What Is Truth?"** Hand in hand with keeping God's Word at the forefront of my mind is disciplining myself to continually ask, "What is Truth?" I picture *Truth* with a capital *T* in my mind to remind myself that, as Christians, we can go to God for divine truth. We don't have to sort through the fake news of social media and the world. We can discipline ourselves to go to the source of truth, which keeps our eyes trained on God and our why rather than on other peoples' opinions and reactions. How often have we seen cancel culture act as judge, jury, and executioner in modern-day life in regard to something most of us will never have all the facts about?

In today's overly connected world of instant communication, it is so easy to form judgments or react to things with only a very small part of the truth. We have to discipline ourselves to ask, "What is Truth?" with the capital *T* so we do not let other peoples' reactions uproot our lives and shake us to our core. Romans 12:2 tells us, "Do not be conformed to this age, but be transformed by the renewing of your mind, so that you may discern what is the good, pleasing, and perfect will of God" (HCSB). If we are living lives worthy of the call God has placed on us, trusting him to stand in the gap of our weakness when we fail forward and forgive us of our sins, it doesn't matter what anyone else thinks.

- **Schedule Time for Spontaneity.** As leaders, we are passionate about our why and what we do. It's part of the reason people want to follow us. That zeal is contagious. But just as I learned in my intentional guided discipline session with my running coach, sometimes I can become too focused and too disciplined. Leaders also need time for fun and spontaneity. I know this is an area of weakness I struggle with, so I began to schedule time for spontaneity. That may sound like an oxymoron. Scheduled spontaneity? However, I realized that having fun was an area of life I wanted to grow in as part of my personal growth plan, so I had to become intentional about putting it in my calendar. Since my husband, Manly, is way better at being spontaneous and fun than I am, I have deferred to his guidance in helping me become more fun and spontaneous.

All these tools can broaden your mind and reframe the way you look at discipline so you can see it in a more positive light. Great leaders learn how to recognize healthy versus unhealthy discipline in order to create sustainable habits that keep them moving onward and upward. They keep their emotions between the lines to create an atmosphere of trust and stability between themselves and their teams, especially when navigating difficult circumstances. They use long-term mind shifts rather than gimmicky mind hacks to take away the fear of strict regimens and routines and replace those extreme tools with more manageable mindsets. And when great leaders plateau in their discipline, they turn to intentional guided discipline by hiring coaches who can objectively assess how to strengthen areas of weakness.

> Great leaders learn how to recognize healthy versus unhealthy discipline in order to create sustainable habits that keep them moving onward and upward.

While there is an economy of exchange associated with discipline as a cost/reward system for achieving long-term goals, when you create a lifestyle of discipline, you actually create a kit filled with a wide array of tools that you can pull from, depending on what kind of discipline you need at a given moment. Having this infrastructure in place not only builds your discipline muscle so it is ready to bolster you when emotions try to take the steering wheel, but it also fosters a lifestyle of freedom that is rooted in what the Bible says about the importance of discipline.

7

Stone 5: Leaders Value Accountability

This is one of my favorite stones to talk about because I am such a big believer in accountability partners. Accountability partners point out personal and professional blind spots—the things you can't see in yourself or are not comfortable addressing in yourself. They push you past your comfort zone, ask great questions, and make you think. Remember that great leaders don't tell you what to do; they teach you how to think. They help you check in with your growth plan, keep you motivated, and keep your emotions between the lines.

Ultimately, leaders need accountability partners to help them become comfortable with the uncomfortable. Life and leadership involve constant change and overcoming adversity, and it helps to have a team to guide, encourage, and keep you accountable, especially as women because we gravitate toward community. So let's build our community of accountability partners together.

> Leaders need accountability partners to help them become comfortable with the uncomfortable.

There are six types of accountability partners that I believe great leaders need: friends, peers, mentors, therapists, trainers, and coaches. Each serves a different purpose for different seasons, but great leaders know the importance of each accountability partner and surround themselves with wise influences. I have often heard the saying "Show me your friends, and I'll show you your future." I love that. It is not enough to just have *any* people in our life. We have to have *wise* people. The Bible even tells us the value of wise counselors: "The one who walks with the wise will become wise, but a companion of fools will suffer harm" (Proverbs 13:20 HCSB).

You become like those you surround yourself with. Do you notice that when you're around your family or friends, your hometown accent becomes thicker, your mannerisms become more exaggerated, and you adopt the dynamic of the environment that you grew up in? It can happen so quickly, almost without thought. We switch back into what is comfortable because, as we've discussed already, our brains crave comfort. If you are blessed to have a positive, encouraging, and uplifting family, this can be a great thing! But I learned a long time ago that there were certain friends and family members that I needed to separate from if I wanted to keep moving onward and upward toward my goals. I made a conscious effort to surround myself with people who had been where I wanted to go and could guide me.

Stepping Stone: Friends

Friends are part of your circle, your "ride or dies" as the kids say. They are the first people you turn to for encouragement and support. They are the ones who make you feel safe and comfortable, the people you risk being transparent with, and the people you trust will protect you and value you, all without a contract!

As someone who has negotiated countless contracts that spell out terms and conditions of a business relationship in an attempt to foresee every possible calamity that could occur between parties, I am amazed that we can form such close relationships based on the unspoken understanding, *I'll be there for you, and you'll be there for me*. These days, most people don't even have that understanding with their own spouse. We get prenuptial agreements to protect ourselves. This isn't to say that friends will always be perfect or won't ever betray us, but having good friends is a crucial part of the human experience.

While friends are fantastic at going through the ups and downs of life alongside you, they are not always the best at holding you accountable. How many times do we, as women, go shopping with our girlfriends and all help each other spend more than we should? I am blessed to have some amazing and hilarious millennial friends. One of them told me that she and her friends love to go on social Target runs. They take a page from the popular sitcom *Parks and Recreation* and encourage each other to "treat yo self" as they group shop and prompt each other to impulse buy things they know they don't need. They call it the magical Target effect. They let Target *tell them* what they need.

Whether or not you've been touched by the magical Target effect, I'm sure there is some area of your life with your friends that you can relate to here. We each have that person who will help us rationalize buying that cute sweater we don't need or decide on the more expensive pair of shoes. My point is that friends can often indulge your emotional impulses or desire for complacency and comfort rather than show tough love to move you toward your life goals. Don't get me wrong; this can be a great thing some of the time. Everyone needs a splurge once in a while. But when you're trying to meet your life goal, friends can too easily let you off the hook rather than encouraging you in your discipline. Their love, compassion, and empathy can cloud their objectivity in helping you reach your goals because they don't want to see you struggle. They want you to "treat yo self!"

Additionally, while friends are great at doing life with you, they don't always have the same goals or experiences to give you specialized advice. They will often give unsolicited advice or do their best to give their opinion, but when they are coming from a field, background, or season of life that is vastly different from where you are or where you're trying to go, friends can be limited accountability partners.

Stepping Stone: Peers

Okay, Dawn, but what about my work friends?

I'm glad you asked! Work friends are your peers, people who are your equals in some way, such as in their background, qualifications, or workplace status. Your peers share similar goals and experiences because they work in the same field or office as you. They often come from comparable educational backgrounds and have complementary skill sets. They are wonderful for collaboration on projects, exchanging ideas, troubleshooting problems in the workplace, and having a shared industry vocabulary that friends outside the workplace may not be familiar with. Peers go through industry situations together and can look at the same task from different technical viewpoints, each offering their unique expertise and experience to achieve a common goal together.

Peers can be better accountability partners for professional situations than friends outside the workplace because of the communal task-oriented environment of the workplace. There is a clear objective, usually a finite time limit to complete the objective, and a sharing of resources and responsibilities among the team members. There is also a degree of pressure associated with not wanting to let your team down. Remember working on group projects back in high school or college? There was always the one person who never turned anything in on time, and the rest of the team was left cramming before the assignment deadline to make up for that one person's lack of effort. In the workplace, there is a greater degree of responsibility and teamwork that keeps peers motivated to work together. Peers will each pull their weight but also keep each other accountable because you are working as equals.

Stepping Stone: Mentors

Mentors are a lot like peers but with a greater degree of success and experience than you currently have in your career. Mentors are the people who get you where you want to go. They have gone through the failing forward process and can educate you to avoid the same mistakes they made. They teach from their own personal experience and are great resources for advice. And because they are in that similar field, they speak the same language that you share with your peers. Plus, mentors are typically in a season of life where they want to give back to the younger generation without charging for their efforts. They have a desire to give of their time, especially where they see talent, leadership, and initiative.

As accountability partners, mentors are those we seek out to teach us and guide us in climbing the ladder of success; however, mentors are not tied to your outcomes. They will talk with you informally and act in an advisory capacity, but it is not their role to help you create and implement systems to keep you on your growth plan. A mentor may meet with you for coffee or set up a phone call to let you pick their brain, but they do not ask you to check in with a report of your success. In a mentor-mentee relationship, both parties walk away having invested little sweat equity.

I don't say this to undermine the value of mentors. Mentors are a crucial part of building that circle for success. When I opened Mochaccinos, having absolutely no idea how to build a coffee shop, I would have failed so fast without other coffee shop owners being willing to mentor me through those early growing pains. I sought out people who ran successful coffee shops anywhere within driving distance and asked them for an hour of their time. I came prepared with all my questions and listened as they shared their experiences. As a result, I was able to avoid many pitfalls of new coffee shop owners. They also introduced me to people in their network and opened doors that I would never have been able to open on my own. But ultimately, it was up to me to implement what I learned in those meetings with my mentors. It was up to me to follow up on the leads they shared and make the calls.

Mentors are also seasonal accountability partners. As you grow, you need to find new mentors who can help you keep growing. The mentors that helped me open my first Mochaccinos were not the same mentors I turned to when I wanted to turn my coffee shop into a franchise. I needed to find new mentors who could guide me through the complex legal paperwork of franchising a business. I had to seek out people who had already been through the process and were willing to pour into me what they had learned so that I could learn from where they had failed forward.

> Mentors are also seasonal accountability partners. As you grow, you need to find new mentors who can help you keep growing.

Finding a mentor is a little bit like playing a game of leapfrog. The mentor helps make it a little easier to jump to that new level of success by learning from their experiences.

Another example of mentorship that I like to use is far less formal. When I first started going to Bible Center Church as a newlywed in Luling, Louisiana, the women in the church took me under their wing and mentored me in being a wife. I had very few healthy marriages modeled to me growing up in the trailer park. And as a new believer, I had no idea what a godly marriage looked like. The ladies in my church taught me how to become a godly wife and mom. They helped me plug into women's Bible studies so I could sit at the feet of the older women and learn what the Scriptures had to say.

I loved how these ladies would open their homes and pull out their good china for us. They believed in using these fine dishes for everyday life as opposed to letting them sit and collect dust in a cupboard. They taught me how to set a table. They showed me how to host wedding and bridal showers for other ladies in the church. I had never been to a real shower in the trailer park. We didn't celebrate things with pride and excellence like I learned from these church ladies.

These were not exceedingly wealthy women. They looked wealthy to me because of how I had grown up, but a lot of their china had been gifted to them at their weddings or passed down from their mothers. My mom didn't have anything of value to give me when I got married, and though my husband and I both worked, we were by no means affluent. These ladies showed me how to thrift, what the millennials now call being "bougie on a budget." I am so grateful for these mentors who taught me how to be a godly woman. They took the time to invest in me and teach me from their own experience so that I could build a godly home and raise a godly family of influence.

While friends, peers, and mentors have all been free accountability partners, now we get into the paid tiers of accountability partners. Think of these as your premium level subscriptions of accountability. You're paying for the luxury of no-commercial access, but now you also have to be ready to do some work.

Stepping Stone: Therapists

Ask anyone who works in real estate, and they'll tell you that the most important part of a house is its foundation. In the same way, before we can start climbing the ladder of success, we need to make sure we have a healthy enough foundation to sustain us. Jesus talked about these two foundations.

> Therefore whoever hears these sayings of Mine, and does them, I will liken him to a wise man who built his house on the rock: and the rain descended, the floods came, and the winds blew and beat on that house; and it did not fall, for it was founded on the rock.

> But everyone who hears these sayings of Mine, and does not do them, will be like a foolish man who built his house on the sand: and the rain descended, the floods came, and the winds blew and beat on that house; and it fell. And great was its fall. (Matthew 7:24–27 NKJV)

In this parable, Jesus illustrates the importance of a strong foundation because he knows the obstacles that life will throw at us. Yet how many of us have examined our foundations? I didn't take a good, long look at mine until I was going through my post-divorce depression. I thought I had built my life on solid rock with my faith—and my faith was still very strong in spite of the emotional pain cave I was going through. However, it wasn't until I began to see a therapist that I realized how the trauma of my childhood had left gaping holes in my foundation that I had ignored and left unaddressed.

My family was a mess. There was poverty, mental illness, disability, and addiction on both sides. I was raising my two younger siblings from the age of ten and working to contribute to our family's finances. I cared for my dad after a stroke left him partially paralyzed and in fits of rage until he died when I was sixteen.

I became financially independent and moved out on my own after graduating high school, working three jobs to put myself through college, and I never looked back. I don't even think I returned home to the trailer park until my grandmother passed when I was an adult. The whole time, I made straight A's and B's, played sports, worked out, and strove to outperform my peers. I had maybe too much discipline from the responsibility placed upon me as a kid, and I became a textbook overachiever. I didn't realize that this was a coping mechanism to avoid dealing with the trauma of my upbringing.

Psychological studies now show that most overachievers suffered childhood trauma that went undiagnosed because it surfaced in behavior that was positively reinforced by adults.[23] Unlike addicts and people who self-medicated in negative ways that attracted concern and adverse attention, overachievers look like well-adjusted, type-A adults. Of course, there are also many healthy type-A adults, but for a number of us, overachieving was or is a way of self-soothing and trying to feel in control.

Even though I had a strong faith, I still needed a therapist to help me fix these holes in my foundation before I could move forward in my growth plan. A therapist is a person who guides you through the pain of the past to heal your foundation. They have psychological training and expertise that you pay for, and in exchange, they teach you how to think differently. They ask questions to make you examine your behavior, and they prompt you to make changes that will keep you moving onward and upward.

> A therapist is a person who guides you through the pain of the past to heal your foundation.

I will be the first to tell you that it is not easy. I had to look at a lot of things in my past that I had buried deep down, but I am so grateful that I did the hard work of therapy because it put me in a much healthier place to achieve a work-life balance.

Had I not realized that I was using work as a coping mechanism, I would not have seen how it was affecting the people around me, including my kids, and I would have continued self-medicating with work. Additionally, had I continued to climb the corporate ladder without addressing the cracks and gaping holes in my foundation, I would have suffered under the responsibilities of increased leadership and the pressure of large-scale decisions. My foundation would not have been able to sustain the success.

Sometimes, it is necessary to take a step backward before you can continue going forward. Therapists are accountability partners that help you fix your foundation.

Stepping Stone: Trainers

Once you have fixed the foundation, then you can start to rebuild. That's where trainers come in. Whereas therapists focus on the past to heal the present, trainers focus on the present to move you into your future. Most often people think of trainers in terms of physical trainers, but trainers can exist in every area of life. They build systems and skills that form new types of "muscles" or habits with a specific end goal in mind. They hold us accountable to a task and often tell us exactly what we need to do in order to accomplish that task. They give instructions for us to follow and expect us to show up and do our part.

Trainers will hold you accountable with metrics that show your progress. From tracking strength gained at the gym month to month or analyzing key performance indicators at the office, a trainer keeps a record of your growth—or lack thereof.

Trainers are another form of paid accountability partners, like therapists, and they are worth the investment. Now you may be tempted to argue with me: "Dawn, I don't need a trainer. I can be disciplined on my own." Hear me out. How often have you started the new year with a resolution to lose weight? You join a gym on January 1, and for those first few weeks of January, it's hard to find a parking place due to all the newly motivated people. But come February 1, the parking lot is empty again. Why? Because even though you're paying the cost of a monthly gym membership, the financial pain point is not high enough to keep you motivated.

Let's just say that a gym membership is $50 a month for an individual. It's easy to do the mental math to justify writing off that investment. *Well, that's really just $2 a day. That's less than a cup of coffee.* The brain is always seeking shortcuts for comfort and complacency.

A trainer, however, is an even bigger investment. And that trainer knows your name, your face, and your goals. They block out time in their schedule just for you, formulate a growth plan with you based on the goals you've shared with them, and they measure results. It's a lot more difficult to justify canceling on a trainer knowing that they're going to charge you regardless of whether you show up or not, and they won't care about your excuses. They've heard them all. They will check in with you and hold you to a higher standard of discipline because you're paying them to. And they get results!

Because they measure your growth over longer periods of time, they will help you consistently amend your growth plan according to what is and is not working by using the cold, hard data they've collected. The numbers don't lie. A trainer will also encourage and keep you motivated when you don't want to show up. They will remind you of your goals and celebrate the victories along the way with you.

Stepping Stone: Coaches

Coaches are the ultimate accountability partners, in my opinion. I am such a big believer in coaches. They possess all the experience and success of a mentor as well as the systems, skills, and metrics of a trainer, but they grow with you for the long haul. Coaches don't tell you what to do like trainers do, but they ask good questions to help you identify your motivation and biases as you work toward your life goals. They help you discover what moves you and what blinds you to success. Now I'm not talking about "life coaches." At least not in the sense of the 2010s phenomenon, when everyone and their brother wanted to become a life coach or consulting guru with no credentials. I'm talking about coaches who command respect in their professional spheres, have a proven track record of both successes and failures, and are continuing to grow and learn themselves.

Now let me clarify: Your CPA is not a coach. Your pastor is not a coach. Your momma who gets medical advice watching daytime TV talk shows is not a coach. Your CPA is someone you usually only meet with once a year to prepare your taxes. Your pastor is not meeting one-on-one with you regularly to put a plan together for how you can move closer to God. Even your general practitioner is someone you may only see for your wellness check, and unless something is wrong, you probably won't be highly motivated to make major life changes. The podcasts you listen to on your commute, while educational and insightful, are not a coach.

A coach is someone who meets one-on-one with you at regular intervals to set goals, create action plans, hold you accountable to those plans, and measure the results. There is direct and personalized communication and accountability between you and your coach that is scheduled and paid for.

> A coach is someone who meets one-on-one with you at regular intervals to set goals, create action plans, hold you accountable to those plans, and measure the results.

So how do you find a coach?

It is so important to do your due diligence when hiring a coach. I cannot tell you the number of people I have met claiming to be business coaches who have never owned a business. Or those who advertise themselves as marriage coaches and have never been married. When I am looking for a coach, I talk to clients they have coached. I will ask a coach to put me in touch with one of their clients whom I can ask about the successes they've had and, more importantly, their failures. I want to know why they failed with their coach and how the coach helped them pick themselves up and learn from the failures to reach success.

I will also ask the same questions to the coach I want to work with. I will ask what they're reading, the podcasts they're listening to, and who's coaching them. I always am suspicious of coaches who do not, themselves, have coaches pushing them to continue growing and striving to meet bigger goals. I will also ask a coach to do a trial session to see how we get along. I don't expect them to do it for free. I want to pay for my coach's time because it is an investment, but before I sign a long-term contract, I do want to ensure we are a good fit. There are tons of great coaches out there, but not every coach is *your* coach.

Spend a little time and money to find your coach because you need to feel comfortable with your coach. You need to have similar communication styles, and you need to make sure your coach has the bandwidth to take you on as a client. You do not want a coach who is already over-scheduled and stretched to their limits. Again, this is a long-term relationship. Talk with them to clearly outline what you expect from each other. Establish how often you are going to check in with each other to revisit your goals and review your progress.

If you think of life as a race, a coach is going to be with you through the training process, at the starting line, beside you each mile of the race, pushing you through the pain cave, crossing the finish line with you, and looking ahead to the next race to repeat the whole process. It is worth the time to find the right coach.

I also believe in having multiple coaches. For every area I want to grow in, I try to find a coach. I've had a nutrition coach, a running coach, a mental toughness coach, a marriage coach, a finance coach, and a spiritual growth coach. I didn't start out having all these coaches at once. I started with the one that was the most important to me at the time and worked within my budget.

Please understand that I am not advocating for you to go into debt to pay for coaches. However, if you really want to grow in a specific area, I encourage you to look at your finances and see where you might be able to allocate money for a coach. Brewing your own coffee instead of paying seven dollars a day for a fancy latte could easily free up the extra money to get you a coach. And because you know what you are giving up as part of a long-term investment in your future, you will be extra motivated to show up and do the work.

Just as we built our discipline kit in the last chapter and filled it with tools, now we are building our team. Having discussed the differences and defined the respective roles among friends, peers, mentors, therapists, trainers, and coaches, it's time for you to start assembling your team. Great leaders have a mixture of people they can turn to in each of these accountability groups. They have friends they can be transparent and unguarded with. They have peers they can collaborate and troubleshoot with. They have mentors they can learn from, therapists who can help them build stronger foundations, trainers who can put systems and plans in place to form new habits, and coaches who will expose their blind spots and grow alongside them for the long haul.

Start surrounding yourself with a team that will help you choose to be 1 percent better, healthier, and more disciplined in achieving your goals every single day.

> Start surrounding yourself with a team that will help you choose to be 1 percent better, healthier, and more disciplined in achieving your goals every single day.

Stone 6: Leaders Communicate Effectively

One of the most underrated qualities of great leaders is their ability to communicate in professional settings. Great leaders can concisely communicate complex ideas to their teams. They understand that time is of the essence and there is little room for miscommunication. They need everyone to know exactly what their goals are and how to complete the plan of attack on deadline. Eloquence is secondary to precision and efficiency.

However, despite women being naturally more communicative than men, women struggle with workplace communication more than men do. Men can boil things down to their most basic essence. They stick to facts and figures. Women like to tell stories and weave emotions to create dramatic tension when they talk. Since we have already discussed that it is important to keep emotions between the lines in the workplace, it is easy to understand how women might have greater difficulty adapting their communication style for the male-dominated world. I am going to give you some tools I have learned to help you become a more disciplined, efficient, and effective communicator in the workplace.

As women, we have had to work twice as hard as our male counterparts not only to achieve the same respect in the workplace but even to earn a seat at the table. We have had to be loud and extra vocal for so long just to be heard and taken seriously. Now, I don't consider myself a radical feminist, but I have been in many board rooms over the years, and I have witnessed firsthand how far things have come just in my lifetime. I went from being the only woman in the room to being surrounded by other smart women leaders. There were many bold women who paved the way for us, and I know I am paving the way for the next generation of women to continue shattering glass ceilings.

Unfortunately, one thing I have observed is that we've been so loud for so long in the workplace that it is now backfiring on us. Now that women have a seat at the table, we must W.A.I.T.

Stepping Stone: First You Must W.A.I.T.

It might seem counterintuitive for me to tell you to W.A.I.T, but W.A.I.T. is an acronym that stands for *Why Am I Talking?* Many times in corporate situations, there is limited time to discuss a preset agenda, and other voices want to share their ideas and data in addition to you. It is critical to read the room and decide if this is the right time and place to share above and beyond what you have been tasked with presenting. Not everything can be addressed in one meeting, and while everyone wants time to contribute fresh ideas to the boss, sometimes you can work against yourself by exceeding your allotted floor time.

Too many times I have left board meetings feeling exhausted by the woman who would not stop talking, the woman who was so desperate to be noticed that she did not take note of the room tone. Instead of delivering what was asked and allowing the next person to speak, she went on rambling tangents, interrupted the other people in the room, brought her personal life into the workplace, or let emotions undermine her own credibility.

Men are very task oriented in the workplace. They want the bottom line delivered as quickly as possible so they can check it off their to-do list and move on to the next thing. If there is a problem that needs to be addressed, men want a straightforward solution. They don't want to waste time talking things out; they just want it fixed.

Women, on the other hand, like to talk things out. We like to process out loud together and will often think nothing of interrupting or talking over one another in group settings. We discuss possible alternatives and think outside the box, not always recognizing that this is something that can be done before or after a meeting. How frustrating it is to go into a meeting and feel like time was wasted and nothing accomplished! This is especially true in the world of post-COVID Zoom meetings.

I know I'm being a little critical of women here, but I have witnessed the men in the room mentally check out when one woman becomes so desperate to be heard that she'll try processing out loud in real time because she is underprepared. Earn the right to have someone's attention by bringing value with every word.

> Earn the right to have someone's attention by bringing value with every word.

In meetings it is critical to stay on topic and be respectful of everyone's time. Before speaking, make sure you are prepared. Make sure you have your facts, figures, and relevant data handy and ready to share as concisely as possible. If you are asked to elaborate, give an opinion, or interpret something in a meeting, then you can expound on your points within reason, but ask yourself, *Why am I talking? Do I have something meaningful to contribute? Am I being mindful of everyone else's time?*

Even if you think sharing an anecdote about your family or friend might illustrate a point, discipline yourself to know the difference between breaktime conversation and "showtime" conversation. Make your case, make it concisely, and let the next person speak.

Stepping Stone: Staying Present and Credible

Remember that women's brains are much more interconnected than men's, so it can be easy for us to drag history into the present. We will look at what has been done in the past and compare the historical scenarios and outcomes to what we are facing now. How many of us do it in our marriages when we argue with our spouse? When we accuse our spouse of acting a certain way that irks us, we go into the annals of our relationship and build a case using ancient history. We think it adds credibility, but in the workplace, it actually undermines our line of reasoning.

Women often tend to look at the past to show patterns that have led to the present. Men don't go historical. They stick to the present and focus on the future. They don't narrativize or catastrophize past circumstances and data trends. They can separate history and emotions from making business decisions.

Where women get into further trouble with workplace communication is when they don't keep their emotions between the lines. Being emotional doesn't always mean crying or shouting or getting too passionate in conversation. Emotions can also get out of boundaries when we exaggerate data in a presentation, overly use superlatives like *best* and *worst* to describe situations, elaborate with too many nonessential details, or rely on too much hearsay and gossip as fact. It is easy for men to discount the credibility and legitimacy of a woman's argument in the workplace if she relies on these emotionally guided conversation tactics rather than coming in with well-researched points and delivering them accurately with poise.

Again, think back to W.A.I.T. Even when you have something worth saying, *how* you say something is almost more important than *what* you're saying. Is your tone even? Women's naturally higher vocal pitches can subliminally affect our credibility. I have had to coach women to lower their tone so that they come across more authoritatively. I've also had to coach women to speak slower and enunciate more clearly. Women who tend to talk quickly can come across as nervous. Their words can become mumbled, which makes them sound unsure of themselves.

We also have to watch our facial expressions and gestures. I get a lot of laughs when I coach women to sit on their hands, especially in negotiations, but our hands can betray us as we talk. When we are demonstrative with our gestures, it can give the impression of being overly emotional, even if we are simply trying to emphasize a point. By physically sitting on your hands, you are presenting a rock-solid stature. You are eliminating superfluous movements that might distract from what you are saying.

The same goes with facial expressions. I know I have a terrible poker face. People can read my face like a book. I have had to really practice disciplining my expressions, and I'm still working on it. My husband and I have known our wonderful business partner, Jill, for many years. Manly has gotten so good at reading her facial expressions that they constantly joke about their ability to have verbally one-sided "conversations." He gets the biggest kick out of saying things to purposefully elicit strong facial reactions from her just to show her how little control she has over her expressions.

Because we women convey so much through nonverbal cues—like hand gestures, facial expressions, tone of voice, and emotionally driven emphases—we have to really discipline and refine the way we present information in the workplace. While these can be positive communication styles outside the workplace, we must do all we can to bolster our credibility through what we say and how we say it in professional settings if we are going to climb the ladder of success.

Stepping Stone: Negotiating Power

Another place where women have struggled in the workplace is in negotiating, particularly with things like salary and benefits. Part of it is that historically, employers have compensated women at a lower rate for the same job men do. Even in 2024, *Forbes Magazine* reports that women earn 16 percent less than their male counterparts or 84 cents to every dollar.[24] Two other important factors are that women don't know how to make the ask nor do they know what to ask for.

Women view negotiation as conflict when, in reality, not every negotiation has to be a contentious discussion. Let's take a moment to reframe negotiation like we reframed discipline.

If you're a parent, I can guarantee you've negotiated with your child or vice versa. Your teen wants to stay out past curfew. Maybe you outright tell them no, but I would venture to say that a lot of times a negotiation ensues, and you end up arriving at a compromise with your child. Now, they might think you're being unfair and adversarial, but as the "boss" in the family dynamic, you know that your child has to prove that they have a good reason for you to relax your boundaries. They have to show maturity to earn your trust that they can handle this privilege, and you both have to be willing to move toward an acceptable middle ground.

In a similar way, negotiation at work is about knowing your worth within a company, being able to demonstrate your worth, knowing what your ideal situation is, and deciding what you're willing to compromise on and what you're not willing to compromise on.

Negotiations don't have to be scary. Having been on both sides of the negotiating table, I know that when a leader finds a good worker with leadership potential, they know it would be foolish not to keep them happy and moving up in the company. However, most women come into the negotiating room unsure of what to ask by way of raises and benefits. They have not compared their role to the median compensation for others in their position, and they are leaning on their emotions and feelings when they make their ask. Without knowing what the market comps are, a lot of women make the mistake of undervaluing or overvaluing their worth. When you undervalue your worth, you leave money on the table. When you overvalue your worth, you need to be prepared to justify the number you've landed on and be willing to compromise.

When members of my team come to me for salary negotiations, one of the first places where they lose me is by telling me how hard they work. Men don't typically use this tactic in negotiating. They assume that everyone is working hard. Women, on the other hand, will get emotional and historical, comparing themselves to other team members and pulling in the "he said/she said" hearsay arguments of how someone else isn't pulling their weight. They'll make lists of times when they feel they've performed beyond their job description instead of showing me how they have contributed to the company.

One way you can assure that a boss will sit up and take notice in a salary negotiation is if you present charts, graphs, KPIs, and data that clearly communicate the value you have brought to the company. Even better is when you can present a growth plan with projections and action plans to continue adding value to the company. Then you make your informed ask using the comps you have researched.

Once you have made your ask—and it is okay to ask for the high range, knowing that you will likely meet somewhere in the middle—you must be willing to be objective. Go into the negotiation knowing your boss will likely not accept your first ask. Put yourself in the boss's shoes. What are some options you might counter with? What options would you be willing to compromise on? Depending on the company you work with, perhaps there are benefits that could offset your salary ask, such as paid time off, retirement options, flexible hours, and so on. Go in knowing what you want and what you will and won't settle for. Be objective, leave your emotions outside the negotiation room, and be willing to advocate for yourself. You are your best ally, especially if you have the data to back you up.

> Be objective, leave your emotions outside the negotiation room, and be willing to advocate for yourself.

Stepping Stone: Where Women Excel in Workplace Communication

I know I've spent the first half of this chapter pointing out areas where women can work to improve their workplace communication skills, but now I want to focus on where women naturally excel.

In *The Female Brain*, Dr. Louann Brizendine, a neuropsychiatrist with degrees from Harvard Medical School, Yale University School of Medicine, and UC Berkeley, studied communication styles between young girls and boys. Young boys gravitated toward games with hierarchies, where they could jockey for position and assert command. Young girls preferred games that were inclusive and peer-based. Instead of giving orders, the young girls would use softer communication phrases such as "'Let's play house'...typically us[ing] language to get consensus, influencing others without telling them directly what to do."[25]

This type of communication prioritizes relationships over tasks, fosters empathy among peers, encourages communal listening, and shows higher emotional intelligence. All these are invaluable communication skills in the workplace and areas where women tend to outperform men.

Women can be just as effective leaders as men because they value relationships and care about team building. It is easy to follow a leader who makes you genuinely feel seen and heard. Women are wonderful at bringing others to the discussion table with that collaborative "let us" invitation that Dr. Brizendine observed. They also more freely give words of affirmation to lift each other up.

Whereas boys are taught to compete from an early age, girls are taught to have fellowship. In most instances, fathers will push boys harder than they will push girls. They encourage their sons to play sports, where there is an automatic focus on competition, winning, and losing. While girls are now encouraged to play sports, parents historically have put them in classes that embraced the arts and did not put as much emphasis on competition. Girls went to dance class, choir practice, and home economic class where they were taught to collaborate with peers and value community. They learned to express themselves as equals without the pressure of determining winners and losers.

In the workplace, these relational communication skills that women are predisposed to from young ages build loyal teams whose members feel like their presence is valued and their roles matter. Women feel more comfortable speaking up because they trust they will be heard and considered without judgment or immediate dismissal. Women also are less likely to talk down to their team members. While we've heard of the term *mansplaining*, which carries the connotation of condescension in communications with men, women are more inclined to teach with empathy.

Merriam-Webster defines *empathy* as "the action of understanding, being aware of, being sensitive to, and vicariously experiencing the feelings, thoughts, and experience of another." Empathy stems from a place of compassion and care. The Bible stresses the importance of empathy: "Rejoice with those who rejoice, and weep with those who weep. Be of the same mind toward one another. Do not set your mind on high things, but associate with the humble. Do not be wise in your own opinion" (Romans 12:15–16 NKJV). When you are sensitive to the feelings of others and can identify with those feelings regardless of whether you have walked a mile in their shoes, you are exhibiting the servant leadership of Christ. I try to embody this type of empathy and servant leadership with my team daily.

> When you are sensitive to the feelings of others and can identify with those feelings regardless of whether you have walked a mile in their shoes, you are exhibiting the servant leadership of Christ.

Listening is part of developing empathy, and it's another highly underrated communication skill at which women excel. Let's be honest.

If you're married, you have probably tried talking to your husband only to realize that he didn't hear a word you said. Women are naturally better at listening and listening actively. Active listening is when you give nonverbal feedback to the person you're listening to that confirms your engagement in the conversation.

Subtle cues like making eye contact, nodding your head, giving little *mm-hmm* affirmations all communicate active listening. They demonstrate humility in that you are willing and able to quiet yourself, prioritize someone else, and give meaningful responses that do not compete with the person talking. Instead of formulating in your head what you're going to say next, you are paying attention to what the other person is saying. This is a skill that great leaders have honed.[26]

Emotional intelligence is another communication skill at which women are more adept than men because women are generally more intuitive when it comes to picking up on nonverbal communication and subtle social cues. Emotional intelligence, or EQ, is comprised of four abilities: self-awareness, self-management, social awareness, and relationship management.[27]

Self-awareness comes from taking an inventory of self: knowing when, where, and how to keep your emotions between the lines in addition to knowing when, where, and how long it is appropriate to command attention in professional group settings. Self-management ties into our earlier discussion of discipline and "includes the quality of self-control, which is the ability to control your emotional reactions."[28]

While women can have a more difficult time recognizing these first two EQ applications (as we discussed in our first two stepping stones of this chapter), women have stronger empathy when it comes to social awareness and relationship management. One aspect of relationship management in which women stand out is the ability to have difficult conversations in order to restore shaky relationships to health.

Stepping Stone: Having Difficult Conversations

In business, you will have difficult conversations. It is unavoidable. When I must have a difficult conversation with a client or someone on my team, I start with reassurance and managing expectations. I am honest that this is not going to be an easy conversation, but I immediately remind them that we are going to get through it together. Then I ask the other person to tell me how I will lose with them and how I will win with them over the course of our conversation. This helps me get to the heart of the issue. The issue they bring to me is usually not really the issue that is bothering them. It's the emotions and fears behind the issue.

For example, once when I asked a coworker to tell me how I would lose with her and how I could win with her, she told me that she perceived I wasn't trusting her. She felt like she was being kept out of key communications on purpose and that I was withholding information from her that would help her do her job. I was so glad she told me this because, from my point of view, that was not at all what was happening. I was trying to spare her from extra emails that I thought were unnecessary notifications. Once I communicated this to her and reassured her that she was a valued and trusted member of the team, the entire mood of the conversation shifted from having an adversarial undertone to carrying mutual respect and understanding.

By the end of our conversation, I knew what she needed to feel validated as a team member, and she understood that I was not excluding her or keeping things from her. I intentionally began to include her on more group communications, knowing it made her feel more secure as a member of my team. This is why communication is so crucial. You never know what is going on in someone's head unless it is verbalized.

> This is why communication is so crucial. You never know what is going on in someone's head unless it is verbalized.

Now, not every problem is as easily solved as this one, but we must be willing to have the difficult conversations, listen to each other, discover how to win and lose with each other, and verbalize how we want to be treated. People don't know how to treat you unless you tell them with respect. When you approach difficult conversations in this way, they turn into empowering conversations and will often go to great lengths to restore relationships with your team.

Just like every other skill we've discussed thus far, communication takes practice and discipline to improve. However, knowing where we, as women, naturally struggle and naturally excel in communicating can go a long way to helping us recognize where we can improve.

One of the easiest ways to improve communicating in the workplace is to ask yourself W.A.I.T.: *Why Am I Talking?* A second way is to stay present and credible. Keep your emotions between the lines and avoid undermining yourself by bringing up ancient history. Focus on the present and negotiate from a position of poise, knowing your value, what you want to ask for, and what you will settle for. Lean into your God-given gifts of emotional intelligence, engaging empathy, active listening, and willingness to restore relationships through difficult conversations.

9

Stone 7: Leaders Prioritize Health

Take a minute to go warm your coffee up or brew a fresh cup. Is it nice and hot? Good. Now settle into your comfy chair and take a sip. We're going to have one of those difficult conversations together. It's not going to feel good, but it's necessary, and we'll get through it.

I want to go back to chapter 5 where we discussed growth plans and planning for retirement. Be honest with yourself. Are you healthy enough physically to enjoy your present life? What about your retirement?

I recently read Dr. Peter Attia's book *Outlive*, and the table of contents stopped me in my tracks. Chapter 1 was titled "The Long Game: From Fast Death to Slow Death."[29] This immediately made me think of my own parents. My dad was a type 1 diabetic who did not take good care of himself. In addition to having a motorcycle accident that left him disabled right after I was born, he had a major stroke when he was thirty-three that left him paralyzed in half of his body. I became his primary caretaker in high school while my mom worked, and I saw the rapid decline in his health before another stroke ultimately claimed his life the day before his thirty-sixth birthday. My mom was diagnosed with breast cancer when I was in my senior year of college and battled it for seventeen years before her death. She also died far too young. Neither of my parents lived long enough to make it to retirement.

In college, I began my long journey of pursuing health. I wanted to not only live to see retirement but also have the quality of life to enjoy it. In a study by the US Census Bureau, not only are Americans living longer today than they were twenty to thirty years ago, but life expectancy is predicted to become greater by 2060. One estimate projects that modern medicine and improvements in technology and quality of care will extend the average age for men by almost nine years.[30] Seeing Dr. Attia's chapter about fast deaths and slow deaths, alongside thinking about my parents, made me realize that health is one of those difficult conversations worth having, especially as leaders and as women.

As leaders, we are tasked with a great deal of responsibility for stewarding resources and shepherding people. If we are not healthy in body, mind, and spirit, we cannot perform at our best. We want to be there to see our kids grow up, get married, and have kids of their own. We need to be healthy to keep up and be active participants in our families so we can enjoy our time with them and not be an added burden. We have people counting on us in our professional and personal lives. It is up to us to be healthy enough to rise to the leadership occasion.

Many people, however, do not realize they are living a slow death because they have not invested in their physical, mental, and spiritual health. We are mind, body, and spirit beings, so we need to take care of all these facets to operate in optimal health. Granted, nobody is guaranteed a tomorrow, but if we want to have our bodies, minds, and spirits well enough to keep up with our long-term goals, we need to start making new healthy habits today. To clarify, this is not going to be one of those weight loss or dieting chapters. This is a *lifestyle* chapter. Let's jump in together.

> If we want to have our bodies, minds, and spirits well enough to keep up with our long-term goals, we need to start making new healthy habits today.

Stepping Stone: Physical Health

I love what Paul said in 1 Corinthians 6:19–20: "Don't you know that your body is a sanctuary of the Holy Spirit who is in you, whom you have from God? You are not your own, for you were bought at a price. Therefore glorify God in your body" (HCSB). Sanctuaries are sacred places designed for fellowship and communion with God, but how often do we treat our bodies with the honor and value they deserve?

We frequently focus on and quote the first half of this verse, but the second half is where we should really sit up and take note. Our bodies are not just divinely created and holy, but they also were bought and paid for by the blood of Christ. When Paul tells us to "glorify God in our body" (HCSB), it is because Genesis 1:27 says that "God created man in His own image" (HCSB), and Christ paid the ultimate price to save us in our current physical bodies for our future spirit bodies.

However, in this day and age of constant busyness, we have become poor stewards of these temples we inhabit. We work too much, don't work out enough, don't get enough sleep, are too tired or busy to properly fuel our bodies, and rely too much on quick processed foods and caffeine to get us through the day. When you add to that the stress of the American lifestyle and the constant overstimulation of screens competing for our attention, is it any wonder that a 2023 Gallup poll shows national anxiety and depression rates at an all-time high?[31]

Whereas a 2020 study by the National Center for Health Statistics showed a consistent year-over-year increase in the consumption of prescription antidepressants and antianxiety medications from 2015 to 2018,[32] a post-COVID study shows rates of prescribed antidepressants and antianxiety medications skyrocketing, particularly among women over the age of twelve.[33] While these meds are incredibly helpful, even lifesaving, in many situations, when I look at these statistics I can't help but wonder how many times these prescriptions jump to treating symptoms before addressing the root issue. As someone who worked in pharmaceutical sales, I know firsthand that the motivating factor of drug manufacturers is not your health; it's the bottom line. They want to sell more and more medications. Again, I'm not against medication, but having spent a lifetime studying health, what if I told you that your physical health is strongly tied to your mental health and vice versa? Increasingly, studies are showing the wonders that physical exercise, nutrition, quality sleep, and giving yourself brain breaks throughout the day have on your mental health.

Let's start with physical exercise. Every time I bring this up when I speak, people come up to me afterward and say, "Dawn, you just don't understand. I don't have time to work out." Okay, but what do you have time for? Do you have time to binge watch several hours of your favorite show at night? Imagine if you had taken just thirty minutes to go for a brisk walk. Do you have time to go get your nails done or your hair colored? I know how many hours we can spend at a hair salon or at the nail salon or simply getting ready each morning. What if you took just fifteen minutes to stretch first or do an online workout? YouTube has plenty of free exercise content you can do from the comfort of your own home with a pair of hand weights. The truth is that you make time for things you consider priorities. What are you prioritizing above your physical health?

> The truth is that you make time for things you consider priorities. What are you prioritizing above your physical health?

It is too easy to make excuses: "I hate working out," "I'm not flexible enough," or "I've tried working out in the past and I didn't lose weight." Or my personal favorite, "Dawn, I just hate sweating." Sweat is the body's way of getting rid of toxins and cooling yourself in the process. Sweat is good for you! Plus, every gym I've ever been to has air conditioning!

Sure, nobody enjoys the soreness after working out when you first begin. The body craves complacency. It wants to stay on the couch. But that soreness means you are moving, and the more you move, the stronger you become. The stronger you become, the less sore you will be. You will have more energy, more flexibility, less pain.

It sounds counterintuitive to work the areas of your body that are causing you pain, but it is often inactivity that creates more pain. Going back to our accountability chapter, this is why trainers are such a great resource. They know how to push you past your comfort zone without hurting you. If you can't afford a personal trainer, find an accountability partner who will go for a walk with you during your lunch break. The worst thing you can do for your body is to stop moving. If you don't use it, you lose it.

I am a huge believer in cross-training. Not only does it prevent boredom with working out, but it also helps your physical state in a variety of areas. I try to rotate cardio, resistance training, and stretching in my weekly workouts. Cardio strengthens your heart, weightlifting or resistance training builds muscle and strengthens your bones—and, let's face it ladies, our bone density takes a hit during menopause—and stretching improves flexibility and balance.

Your physical exercise regimen does not have to be extreme. Just as sustainability is key with all discipline, it's also key with health-related discipline. Find a workout you enjoy, and if you don't know what you enjoy, try a bunch of different things. If you hate sweating, most treadmills now have personal fans you can blast to your heart's content. Try a kickboxing class or a dance class if you hate walking on a treadmill. I can guarantee you there is an exercise out there you will enjoy if you make it a priority to find one. There will always be an excuse not to do something, but what are those excuses costing the state of your temple in the long run?

> There will always be an excuse not to do something, but what are those excuses costing the state of your temple in the long run?

In addition to physical exercise, nutrition is of equal importance. When I say *nutrition*, I am not talking about *diets*. To me, *diet* is a four-letter word. They do not work. They are often quick-fix fads that are unhealthy long-term. Diets are like the mind hacks we discussed in chapter 6. They only get you so far until you see they are unsustainable for long periods of time. They focus on deprivation and giving things up rather than putting good things in. Nutrition, on the other hand, is like the mind shift or, in this case, a lifestyle shift. It is sustainable and requires making changes to your lifestyle and reframing how you think about food in terms of good, clean, healthy fuel.

Think of the numerous supermodels who look like the epitome of beauty because they are so thin. Sometimes, though, they are unhealthy. They might be skinny, but they are doing long-term damage to their bodies by what they are putting into them (or not putting into them). You can be skinny and still have higher fat than muscle content. Women naturally carry more visceral fat than men, and it is the visceral fat that causes heart problems later in life.[34] Instead, I think of nutrition in terms of food as fuel. If you want to fuel your body for good performance, you have to put good things into it.

Nutrition focuses on health and growth. It is not directly tied to weight, although weight is a factor. Rather than only focusing on calories, nutrition focuses on what comprises those calories. The body needs healthy fats, protein, carbohydrates, and fiber. Healthy fats promote brain functioning, protein helps cells rebuild and heal, carbohydrates provide energy, and fiber keeps our gut healthy. Nutrition also places importance on foods that are high in vitamins and minerals which aid all of the different body systems so they function more efficiently. Of course this is an oversimplified breakdown of nutrition, but it is a place to start when you decide to examine how you are feeding your temple.

Again, when I talk about nutrition, I am met with a lot of excuses, mostly tied to peoples' lack of time to cook in their busy schedules. I get it. I was a working single mom with three kids for a number of years. If there was one thing I didn't have, it was extra time. But I will remind you of how I answer people who say they don't have time to exercise: what are you doing with your time that is more important than long-term health? I knew that I wouldn't have time to cook dinner every day between work, homeschooling my kids, *and* taking them to sports practice and games, so I had to budget my time. I planned my meals and prepped them in advance. I got things that were quick and easy to cook but still had nutrition, and I would freeze them to reheat throughout the week.

To this day, I still do meal prep because even though my kids are grown and out of the house, I often work late, get home and go for a walk or light run with my husband, and want the convenience of heating something up in the microwave. (We are currently falling in love with the air fryer). Meal prep not only ensures I have something healthy to eat when I am busy, but it also helps me control the calories I am eating, provides my body with macro- and micro-nutrients to keep me performing well in the high-stress environment I work in, and helps me avoid giving into the cravings for quick carbs when hunger hits. I have done this long enough to know my go-to recipes that I enjoy preparing and eating throughout the week, and I feel so much better when I am disciplined with what I eat. When I do go out and splurge on a meal, I definitely feel the difference the next day. My mind is clearer, and there is less inflammation and water retention when I cook for myself and focus on good, clean nutrition.

The last part of my physical health regimen is sleep and brain breaks. Like most Americans, I am tied to my phone far more than I wish I were. It is always with me, always notifying me of things competing for my attention. Most of the time, these notifications are not pressing and can be taken care of at a later time, but there is still that temptation to mindlessly scroll through social media.

How many hours do we waste scrolling that we could be putting toward our physical health with exercise, nutrition, and sleep? I realized that I had to become disciplined at putting the phone down to give myself brain breaks throughout the day. I also had to create a new sleep routine that involved putting the phone on "do not disturb" and reading a book instead.

I will take breaks throughout my day by putting my phone down or stepping away from the computer and going on a five-minute walk around my office park just to clear my head. I don't play music. I don't text or talk to people on the phone. I just enjoy the silence. If I feel the need to talk to someone, I will pray. These small breaks do wonders for my physical, mental, and spiritual health.

At night, I turn the TV off and put the phone away at least an hour before I plan to go to sleep. There is increasing data about the blue light from electronic screens harming our sleep cycles, and sleep is when the body does most of its healing. A Harvard Health Study in 2020 showed how blue light disrupts the body's natural circadian rhythm that helps us fall asleep, stay asleep, and have quality restorative sleep.[35]

Without sleep, our mental health, emotional health, and physical health suffers. Insufficient sleep can even compromise our immune systems and make us more prone to colds. Sleep is so important to our minds and bodies that it is worth the discipline of putting the screen away so you can settle into a relaxed brain state. When we think of our physical bodies, we have to consider our brains, which work so hard. They need a break too! Between physical exercise, nutrition, sleep, and giving yourself brain breaks, you will be on your way to improving your physical health.

Stepping Stone: Mental Health

Your physical health is closely tied to your mental health. If you do a deep dive into the science of hormones and body chemistry, you'll find that physical exercise is one of the most effective ways to combat anxiety and depression because it affects the hypothalamus, the part of the brain that controls hormones.[36] Exercise, or any vigorous movement, releases endorphins and endocannabinoids that create the effect of a "high" in the brain.[37] Have you ever heard of a "runner's high"? It is the natural good feeling that comes after a cardio workout. Exercise can also release the hormone dopamine in the brain, which promotes feelings of calm. Exercise further releases stress (cortisol) that is stored in the muscles, and it increases the oxygen supply to the brain to promote greater neuroplasticity and clearer thinking.[38] Overall, exercise is a simple way to see vast improvement in your mental health.

Now, let me qualify all this by emphasizing that I am not a doctor. I am not credentialed to give medical advice. I am simply a lifelong student of health with a degree in biology, a minor in chemistry, and an early career in pharmaceutical sales. I am not against antidepressants or antianxiety medications, but I feel like we, as a society, are so overmedicated. My opinion is that doctors are too quick to prescribe medications because of the pressure and kickbacks they receive from pharmaceutical companies. Today, people stay on these powerful medications for years, and their bodies become dependent to the point where it is difficult to get off the meds.

Without trying to sound like a conspiracy theorist, the drug companies know that the longer they can keep you medicated, as I said at the beginning of this chapter, the bigger the profit they can make. Their motives for making you feel better are not entirely pure. Now, of course, you should *never* make any changes to your medication without speaking to your healthcare professional first, but I am a huge advocate for looking for natural ways to care for your long-term mental health.

Again, I am a self-proclaimed health nerd. I love reading about the science of the body and the mind. In the endnotes of this book, you can see where to find every study that I am quoting to do your own research. However, I am about to introduce you to several techniques that have strong scientific data—and are backed by Scripture! Over the years I have found that these techniques have helped improve my mental health: therapy, gratitude, journaling, deep breathing, and meditation. These are things I have in my mental health tool kit and have disciplined myself to practice since going through my mental health battle as well as coming from a family with history in depression, anxiety, addiction, and bipolar syndrome.

Therapy is the first tool that can help immensely with mental health. I discussed this a little bit in chapter 7 in relation to our accountability partners. Therapy is both scientifically and scripturally backed. The Bible says, "Plans fail when there is no counsel, but with many advisers they succeed" (Proverbs 15:22 HCSB). We are planning for our long-term well-being so that we can have the quality of life we need to fulfill our purpose and enjoy our retirement, right? The Bible tells us that without advisers, of which counselors and therapists are examples, those plans have a higher chance of failure.

Scripture also tells us, "The purpose in a man's heart is like deep water, but a man of understanding will draw it out" (Proverbs 20:5 ESV). I love this translation of this verse. Think about deep waters like oceans. The metaphor here is so fantastic because our psyches are just like the oceans. They can be dark with strong undercurrents. According to National Geographic, over 80 percent of the oceans on planet earth are still unmapped.[39] The same is true for our minds. We don't even know what we don't know about ourselves, the things buried deep in our hearts and memories, especially when there is trauma, betrayal, abuse, or fear. Without a therapist to help you explore these deep, dark places, the strong undercurrents of those mental wounds can negatively affect your mental health, your ability to fulfill your purpose, and your ability to effectively lead others. A wise and credentialed therapist can draw these hidden things out, help you manage the stress and anxiety of life, guide you through periods of depression, and positively re-form the way you think.

Gratitude is the second tool that has scriptural and scientific backing as a means of combating depression. A study by UC Berkeley shows that "people who consciously count their blessings tend to be happier and less depressed."[40] Paul wrote in Philippians 4:6–7, "Don't worry about anything, but in everything, through prayer and petition with thanksgiving, let your requests be made known to God. And the peace of God, which surpasses every thought, will guard your hearts and minds in Christ Jesus" (HCSB). The apostle Paul knew that gratitude, thankfulness, and counting your blessings would bring peace, and now science is backing it up with concrete data. The UC Berkeley study revealed that people who took time for gratitude journaling every day for twelve weeks in addition to regular counseling had significantly better mental health improvement than another group in the study who received counseling and wrote about their negative feelings.[41] In a different study by Harvard Health, research demonstrated that "in positive psychology research, gratitude is strongly and consistently associated with greater happiness. Gratitude helps people feel more positive emotions, relish good experiences, improve their health, deal with adversity, and build strong relationships."[42]

In my personal life, I am a huge fan of gratitude journaling. I have used *The Five Minute Journal* from Intelligent Change for ten years. I love it because it is an intentional, guided gratitude journal for the morning before you start your day and the evening when you reflect on your day. It literally takes five minutes at the open and close of each day to focus your mind on things you are grateful for. Gratitude is one of those mind shifts in which you can discipline yourself, training your mind to look for the positive and appreciate the little things, and it also releases those good hormones: "When we express gratitude and receive the same, our brain releases dopamine and serotonin, the two crucial neurotransmitters responsible for our emotions, and they make us feel 'good.'"[43]

The icing on the gratitude cake is that in addition to the many benefits it brings to our own mental health, studies show it also makes us better, more empathetic leaders. Gratitude makes leaders more "compassionate, considerate, empathetic, and loved among others," according to research cited by Positive Psychology.[44] When you are grateful, people are drawn to you.

> When you are grateful,
> people are drawn to you.

Deep breathing is a third tactic that promotes relaxation and can decrease anxiety. "Deep breathing" is a more colloquial name for *diaphragmatic breathing*, breath that fills the lungs down to the diaphragm. The National Cancer Institute explains that deep breathing helps "boost the amount of oxygen in the blood, lowers blood pressure and heart rate, and reduces muscle tension."[45] It also helps the brain move from operating in the sympathetic nervous system to the parasympathetic nervous system.

The Cleveland Clinic defines the difference between the sympathetic and parasympathetic nervous systems as follows: "Your sympathetic nervous system carries signals that put your body's systems on alert, and your parasympathetic carries signals that return those systems to their standard activity levels."[46] I frequently practice non-sleep deep rest (NSDR), which combines deep breathing with a guided meditation that helps transition the brain from operating in the sympathetic nervous system to the parasympathetic nervous system.

I was first introduced to NSDR through health and science podcaster Andrew Huberman. I was going through some very hectic and stressful times during my transition to a new job that relocated me and my family from southeast Louisiana to North Atlanta. I was on the verge of burnout and badly in need of rest when I came across one of Huberman's YouTube videos that offer a ten-minute guided NSDR meditation. I wasn't totally convinced it would work as advertised, but I was desperate, so I tried it.

Huberman explains that NSDR is supposed to "guide your brain and body into a state of deep relaxation without falling asleep completely."[47] I certainly did not have time for a nap. It was all I could do to take ten minutes to try this video, but let me tell you, I was blown away by the results. In ten minutes, I felt like I had taken a three-hour nap. I had energy, my brain was clear, and I was so much more productive afterward. It made me realize how badly our brains need a break just like our bodies do.

In today's highly competitive, high-stress environment, where we are glued to our electronic devices and constantly bombarded with communication notifications, our brains have been trained to stay in the sympathetic, or high-alert, stage. But that is not how God designed our brains to function. The sympathetic nervous system was designed for protection when we are in danger. It activates the fight-or-flight burst of adrenaline hormone, and when we stay in the sympathetic nervous system for prolonged periods of time, it increases anxiety and fatigue, leading to burnout.[48] Deep, diaphragmatic breathing helps the mind and body transition from the high-alert sympathetic nervous system to the calming parasympathetic nervous system.

Again, I love it when science backs up Scripture, and the Bible says, "This is what the Lord God says to these bones: I will cause breath to enter you, and you will live" (Ezekiel 37:5 HCSB). God created us as breathing creatures, so he knows that breath is essential to reviving our bodies and bringing fresh life. Deep breathing is the best way to fully absorb this life-giving gift of God. I cannot encourage you enough to take a few minutes throughout the day to just breathe in that life. It will do wonders for your mental and physical health.

The last tactic for mental health that I am a big proponent of is meditation. Now hang on; before you start saying, "Dawn, I was following you, but meditation? Isn't that new-agey? Really?" Yes, really, and I can point to Scripture to back this up. We've reframed a couple things already, let's reframe this too. First, let's look at the definition of *meditation*, because like *discipline*, it should not be a scary word. Dictionary.com defines meditation as "continued or extended thought; reflection; contemplation" and "devout religious contemplation or spiritual introspection."

At its core, meditation is a practice of thinking about what you're thinking about, which is scriptural. The Bible tells us that we should be "bringing every thought into captivity to the obedience of Christ" (2 Corinthians 10:5 NKJV). In other words, we should be thinking about what we're thinking about and making sure it is in line with what God says. That includes the practice of meditation.

> At its core, meditation is a practice of thinking about what you're thinking about, which is scriptural.

When David wrote the Psalms, he was practicing meditation. "May my meditation be sweet to Him; I will be glad in the LORD" (Psalm 104:34 NKJV). David asked that his meditation be accepted and approved by God. Elsewhere, he said "Oh, how I love Your law! It is my meditation all the day" (119:97 NKJV). This verse explains that David meditated by thinking about God's Word, the law, and thinking about it all throughout the day.

Our practice of meditation can glorify God through thinking about his Word, memorizing Scripture, and praying. It can be a mix of deep breathing, gratitude journaling, listening to worship music—anything that focuses your mind off yourself and your problems and takes your thoughts into captivity. In meditation, you can do what Peter urged by "casting all your care upon Him, for He cares for you" (1 Peter 5:7 NKJV). You can share your anxieties with God and receive his perfect peace (Isaiah 26:3).

Science also confirms that meditation lowers stress and is another means of transitioning your body from the sympathetic nervous system to the parasympathetic nervous system. Meditating decreases anxiety, increases brain clarity, lowers blood pressure, and can fight depression because it gets you into the habit of taking your thoughts captive and thinking about what you're thinking about. Meditation is another mind shift that forms new healthy habits that improve mental and spiritual health.

Stepping Stone: Spiritual Health

The last area of health is your spiritual health. It is arguably the most important form of health after which your physical and mental health will fall in line. When you put God first as part of your routine, you are admitting to yourself that you are not in control. You are trusting God to be in control and committing to ride alongside him in the passenger seat. Talk about taking the pressure off your shoulders!

> When you put God first as part of your routine, you are admitting to yourself that you are not in control. You are trusting God to be in control.

Jesus said, "Do not worry, saying, 'What shall we eat?' or 'What shall we drink?' or 'What shall we wear?' for after all these things the Gentiles seek. For your heavenly Father knows that you need all these things. But seek first the kingdom of God and His righteousness, and all these things shall be added to you" (Matthew 6:31–33 NKJV). We can find comfort knowing that God knows what we need more than we do. Even more so, he has promised to provide these things to us, but first we need to seek him.

My spiritual health plan includes journaling, prayer, reading devotions, memorizing Scripture, and taking sabbaticals. I've already discussed my gratitude journaling practice and how that helps me start and end the day with thankfulness. I've also talked about how I use meditation as a time for prayer and reflection. There is a lot of overlap between the things we do for our physical, mental, and spiritual health because God designed us as physical, mental, and spiritual beings. We cannot thrive unless we are working on all three, and often what is good for one part of our three-part being is good for the other parts.

The third thing that I do for my spiritual health—and something I believe we do not prioritize enough—is memorizing Scripture. When we take the time to memorize Scripture, it is ready for us when we need it. It is part of our spiritual armor, how we fight against physical, mental, and spiritual obstacles. It is the sword of the Spirit that Ephesians 6:17 talks about, our offensive weapon. However, you cannot use a weapon you do not have. If you forget your sword at home, it is ineffective.

Memorizing Scripture ensures we carry our sword with us at all times and that it is sharp and ever at the ready. The Bible says, "This book of instruction must not depart from your mouth; you are to recite it day and night so that you may carefully observe everything written in it. For then you will prosper and succeed in whatever you do" (Joshua 1:8 HCSB). God gives us such a wonderful promise in this verse. If we do our part and memorize Scripture, meditate on it, and carry it with us, we will be successful. We will be equipped because we have strengthened our spiritual muscles and improved our spiritual health.

The final thing I do for my spiritual health is take sabbaticals. *Sabbatical* comes from the word *sabbath*, which means "to rest." I view sabbaticals as preventive spiritual care, kind of like going to the dentist to prevent cavities. I will dive deeper into sabbaticals in chapter 15 when we discuss faith, but I want to introduce the concept here.

When I take a sabbatical, I go away somewhere, usually to my cabin, and I get alone with God. I use it as a period of rest, reflection, prayer, fasting, and listening for the Lord to speak to me. I follow Moses' example when he went up to the mountaintop to get alone with God before he received the Ten Commandments in Exodus. I turn off all my electronic devices to prevent distractions and give my brain a break. The only things I bring with me are my Bible and a journal. I will go for long walks and pray, but I will also sit, quiet myself, and *listen* for God to talk to me. I try to do this at least every quarter because I know how refreshed I am when I come back. A sabbatical brings me closer to God and it improves my mental and spiritual health. I am able to recharge, refocus, and better lead my team.

As we get to the end of this chapter, I know I have thrown a lot at you. I know it might be a bit overwhelming, but I am asking you to start taking your health seriously. Treat your body like the temple that God designed it to be. We are striving for 1 percent better each and every day, right? What do you have to do *today* to be 1 percent healthier than yesterday? Start building the little wins. Add a five-minute walk in the middle of your day, give yourself a ten-minute brain break, and spend a few minutes winding down with gratitude. That's not even half an hour out of your busy day, but it will do wonders for your physical, mental, and spiritual health.

I didn't begin getting up at 4:44 a.m. and going for twelve-mile runs, but just like with our growth plans, our health goals grow with us as we become more disciplined. I knew that if I wanted to have time for my physical, mental, and spiritual health, it would require getting up early, but I would feel so much better as a result. I started doing this when my kids were little and I was a working, homeschooling single mom. I would always get up way before my kids so that I could be rested, spiritually fed, physically fit, and ready for my day as a single parent. Now, it continues to be part of my daily routine. I start each morning with my prayer and meditation time, do my five-minute gratitude journal, read my Bible and devotional, *have some coffee*, and then go for my morning run. That way, by the time I arrive at the office, my body, mind, and spirit are all fed. I enter the office focused, ready to lead my team and face any obstacles that arise.

I have also invested into my long-term physical, mental, and spiritual health so that I can, God-willing, reach retirement age in a state to enjoy the fruits of my hard work in ways that my family never did. If you are not living the quality of life you desire, I encourage you to ask yourself, *What changes do I need to make today to get myself 1 percent closer to where I want to be?* Then stop making excuses and *do it*. Your team will thank you, and you will thank yourself later.

Stone 8: Leaders Grow in Wisdom

One thing I've observed about leaders over the years is that the truly great ones possess wisdom. I have always admired wisdom as a character trait and pray for it daily in my own life. In this chapter, I want to discuss wisdom for women in the workplace. We often use *knowledge* and *wisdom* as interchangeable terms, but they are two different concepts. I like to think of knowledge as being "book smart" and wisdom as being "street smart." Knowledge is intellectual; it's a list of facts. It comes from being a good student of a particular subject or subjects. There is usually a lot of memorization and research involved in gaining knowledge.

Wisdom, on the other hand, is more experiential and applied. When you are wise, it is part of your state of being. Wisdom comes from life, from trial and error, from risking and failing, and developing the ability to make good choices. It is deeply tested over time and applied across multiple spheres of life, but most importantly, it leaves a legacy for others to follow.

While people who are wise may also be knowledgeable in their fields, not everyone who possesses knowledge is wise. You can even have high intelligence but not be wise. With wisdom, we say that someone *is* wise. With knowledge, we usually say that someone *has* knowledge in a particular field. It is limited in scope. "Oh, he's knowledgeable in medicine" or

"She's knowledgeable in history." We don't assign field specificity to wisdom. You either have it or you don't. You can become knowledgeable in something relatively quickly. Wisdom takes time and maturity to develop.

> Wisdom takes time and maturity to develop.

Wisdom is an ability to take knowledge and apply it to different situations. There is an interconnected approach to living, leading, and problem-solving associated with wisdom. Usually someone who has wisdom can absorb data, see historical patterns, observe present challenges, and interpret these factors to learn from the past and create an innovative approach for present-day situations.

While some people seem to naturally possess wisdom, no one is born wise. I firmly believe wisdom is something that any leader can grow in and develop just like the other Stones we've discussed. But, like the other Stones we've talked about, it takes time and discipline. Before we can grow in wisdom, we must learn to recognize its signs.

Stepping Stone: Recognizing Wisdom

There is no better place to start learning about wisdom than the book of Proverbs. God loved David so much that when his son Solomon became king of Israel, God was prepared to honor Solomon with whatever he wanted. Out of everything Solomon could have asked God for, he asked for wisdom.

James 1:5 tells us that this is a prayer God still honors today: "If any of you lacks wisdom, let him ask God, who gives generously to all without reproach, and it will be given him" (ESV). I've already shared how wisdom is something I pray for daily, and I am continually amazed at how God gives me wisdom when I need it. I also repeatedly read the book of Proverbs as part of my spiritual health. It is the legacy of godly wisdom that Solomon left behind for us to learn from, and I dedicate a great deal of time studying and memorizing this particular book of the

Bible. I want my sword of the Spirit to be rich in verses about wisdom when I need it.

While there is such a thing as secular wisdom, spiritual wisdom is on a whole different level because it comes from the Creator of the universe, who is omniscient, all-knowing in every way. That's the kind of wisdom I want to learn from. "The Lord gives wisdom; from His mouth come knowledge and understanding" (Proverbs 2:6 NKJV). Not only is Solomon explicitly telling us how to get wisdom—directly from God, the source of all wisdom—but he is also sharing that if we ask God for wisdom, we will get knowledge and understanding too.

It's like one of those infomercials you see on TV: "But wait! There's more!" In addition to telling us where to get wisdom and how to recognize wisdom, Scripture explains that there are promises and gifts that come with desiring wisdom: "Happy is a man who finds wisdom and who acquires understanding, for she is more profitable than silver, and her revenue is better than gold. She is more precious than jewels; nothing you desire compares with her. Long life is in her right hand; in her left, riches and honor. Her ways are pleasant, and all her paths, peaceful. She is a tree of life to those who embrace her, and those who hold on to her are happy" (Proverbs 3:13–18 HCSB).

Happiness, long life, riches, honor, and peace—these are all promises that God says come with wisdom. Yes please! Can I get some coffee with that too? Unlike silver, gold, and jewels, wisdom does not tarnish but grows with age and experience. It can't be stolen. So how do you recognize wisdom? Proverbs tells us that too. "Listen to counsel and receive instruction so that you may be wise later in life" (19:20 HCSB).

> Happiness, long life, riches, honor, and peace—these are all promises that God says come with wisdom.

Eastern cultures like those in China and Japan have a reverence for the elderly. Their families, communities, and societies value the wisdom the elderly have gained through their long lives. Even in many southern European countries like Italy and Greece, where it is common for multiple generations to dwell under the same roof, grandparents pour their wisdom into the younger generations. "Wisdom is found with the elderly, and understanding comes with long life" (Job 12:12 HCSB). It takes wisdom to survive and live a long life.

Our modern American culture is unique in that it places such importance on youth and self, and I personally believe it does us a disservice. "The global anti-aging market was valued at around 62 billion U.S. dollars in 2021 and is expected to increase to some 93 billion by 2027."[49] Those are shocking statistics! However, at many speaking engagements, I see the evidence of those stats when I ask a question that causes many women to bristle: "How much did you spend on Botox last year versus books or courses?" Of course no one rushes to answer, so I'll usually follow up with another question that doesn't exactly increase my popularity at that moment: "How many of you could have hired a coach with the time and money you spent at the hair salon or the nail salon this year?"

It's one of those difficult conversations, but it makes women think. Not that men aren't guilty of vanity, but women tend to be far more prone to it. And I'll admit I'm not immune, but I have learned the value of investing in things that bring long-term gain, like wisdom, rather than short-term gratification. (I literally got an invitation from a friend to a Botox and filler party as I was writing this manuscript. I earned these wrinkles, thank you very much!)

Now I know I'm being a little facetious here poking fun at this topic. I'm certainly not saying that you shouldn't care about your appearance or never get Botox—I certainly do take care of my external appearance as part of stewarding my bodily temple!—but you should take inventory of where you are allocating your time and resources. There is, of course, a balance to everything in life, but my point is ultimately to not let concern over your appearance or chasing the fountain of youth cross over into vanity and pride at the expense of building wisdom and character that helps you reach your life goals.

Proverbs 31:30 warns of vanity: "Charm is deceitful, and beauty is vain, but a woman who fears the Lord is to be praised" (ESV). Proverbs also explains that "The fear of the Lord is the beginning of wisdom, and the knowledge of the Holy One is understanding" (9:10 HCSB). If we, as women, put more time, effort, and money into growing in wisdom than we do in trying to avoid wrinkles, gray hair, and cellulite, it would benefit us so much more internally. Consider what is being spent on a physical shell compared to what you are spending time-wise, energy-wise, and money-wise on bettering your future quality of life, achieving your goals, and walking in your God-given purpose here on earth. Be willing to apply wisdom.

We gain wisdom from listening to others who have wisdom to pass down, like mentors, trainers, and coaches. We gain wisdom from experts through books, podcasts, conferences, and continuing education courses. We gain wisdom from experiences and fellowship, and from prayer and Bible reading. Eastern and European cultures pass down a legacy of wisdom through discussion. They recognize that it is more important for the younger generations to listen and learn than to be constantly trying to prove their intelligence.

In chapter 8 on communication, we talked about the importance of listening. Really listening. Not just being quiet long enough to formulate in your head what you're going to say next, but really paying attention to what others around you are sharing from their experience and knowledge.

We've already talked about how too many women in the workplace do not know when to stop talking and W.A.I.T. Thinking twice before speaking is a scriptural concept. "The intelligent person restrains his words, and one who keeps a cool head is a man of understanding. Even a fool is considered wise when he keeps silent, discerning when he seals his lips"

(Proverbs 17:27–28 HCSB). I've seen so many intelligent women come across as foolish know-it-alls because they didn't practice self-control long enough to stop talking and listen. Solomon wrote that even a fool *appears* wise if he isn't always running his mouth. I've also observed that usually the wisest person in the room is the one saying the least, the one sitting back and observing, taking everything in, considering the information being given, and looking at its greater application.

Another way to recognize wisdom is through practicing humility. The people showboating and tooting their own horns are often not as wise as they think they are. Humility illustrates wisdom because it is not vainglorious. Humility lifts others up, makes sacrifices, and realizes there is always room to learn more. "When pride comes, disgrace follows, but with humility comes wisdom" (Proverbs 11:2 HCSB). Pride is selfish; humility is selfless. Even when you are put in a position of leadership where you are sometimes expected to do a lot more of the talking and receive a lot more of the praise, wise leaders practice humility by sharing the credit with their teams. They realize they could not have gotten to their position alone. Success does not happen in a vacuum. Wisdom recognizes that and gives credit where credit is due, according to what Paul wrote: "Pay to all what is owed to them: taxes to whom taxes are owed, revenue to whom revenue is owed, respect to whom respect is owed, honor to whom honor is owed" (Romans 13:7 ESV).

> Wise leaders practice humility by sharing the credit with their teams.

As a whole, Proverbs is packed full of practical examples of how we can recognize and grow in wisdom. Proverbs 31 is even completely dedicated to women. I know this can be a controversial chapter to discuss in today's climate of gender politics and radical feminism, but if we look at the heart of Proverbs 31, it is not intended to keep women back or set us up for failure. Quite the opposite! Proverbs 31 inspires me because it gives me a role model to look up to. It is the ideal woman as God sees her. It can be easy to get hung up on the "Virtuous Wife" title that the NKJV translation uses and become myopic in thinking that the Proverbs 31 woman only applies to married women in the home, but let's look at this closer because, again, that is such a limited perspective to take on this chapter.

When I read Proverbs 31, I see a wife, mom, philanthropist, and businesswoman! Who wouldn't want to embody the wisdom of the Proverbs 31 woman? This chapter, to me, shows how richly God values women. Let's look at the following verses:

> She brings her food from afar. She also rises while it is yet night, and provides food for her household, and a portion for her maidservants. She considers a field and buys it; from her profits she plants a vineyard. She girds herself with strength, and strengthens her arms. She perceives that her merchandise is good, and her lamp does not go out by night. She stretches out her hands to the distaff, and her hand holds the spindle. She extends her hand to the poor, yes, she reaches out her hands to the needy. She makes tapestry for herself; her clothing is fine linen and purple. Her husband is known in the gates, when he sits among the elders of the land. She makes linen garments and sells them, and supplies sashes for the merchants.
> (Proverbs 31:14–24 NKJV)

Verse 16 shows us that the Proverbs 31 woman is a real estate investor. She buys land and builds a business. In verses 22–24, she sells her wine and the textiles she produces. This shows me that the Proverbs 31 woman is an entrepreneur in multiple fields. Verses 15 and 20–21 tell us that not only does she have people working under her that she provides for and pays, but she also is a philanthropist in the community, caring for the poor and the needy. This woman has a busy life in addition to having a husband and children. She's the ultimate supermom, and the Bible praises this and calls her wise. This woman has large influence personally, professionally, and socially.

The New Testament honors another businesswoman when Luke writes about Lydia the textile merchant:

> We were staying in [Philippi] for some days. And on the Sabbath day we went out of the city to the riverside, where prayer was customarily made; and we sat down and spoke to the women who met there. Now a certain woman named Lydia heard us. She was a seller of purple from the city of Thyatira, who worshiped God. The Lord opened her heart to heed the things spoken by Paul. And when she and her household were baptized, she begged us, saying, "If you have judged me to be faithful to the Lord, come to my house and stay." So she persuaded us. (Acts 16:12–15 NKJV)

Though not as much is said about Lydia as about the Proverbs 31 role model for women, the Bible not only honors Lydia as a prominent businesswoman at a time when women were not highly regarded in society, but it also credits her as one of Paul's first baptized converts.

An article by the NIV Bible blog[50] provides a little extra historical context for this short passage in the Bible, stating that Lydia was an importer of the most valuable and expensive purple dye for textiles at the time. Lydia had wealth, and more than that, she was an international businesswoman, negotiating with producers and merchants to sell this pricey commodity. To deal with men from other regions, she had to be shrewd and wise.

Luke could have merely referred to Lydia as a convert to early Christianity, but instead he honored her by recognizing her position and influence. In addition to finding personal salvation through her dealings with Paul, Lydia influenced her entire household to find Christ.

That is our ultimate why as businesswomen. Sure, it is wonderful to be successful and build businesses, but if we are not living for Christ, then what is the purpose? We can't take it with us. Yet other souls will have eternal life because of our integrity, our leadership, and our ability to communicate God's love. That is wisdom that leaves a legacy. The book of Proverbs, the Proverbs 31 woman, and the story of Lydia all show the influence we can have on this earth and for heaven when we recognize and grow in wisdom.

> Other souls will have eternal life because of our integrity, our leadership, and our ability to communicate God's love. That is wisdom that leaves a legacy.

Stepping Stone: Applying Wisdom and Knowledge in the Workplace

Now that we know what wisdom is and how to recognize it, it's time to apply it to the workplace. Leaders carry so much responsibility, especially in the workplace, that they need much wisdom to manage day-to-day decisions. This doesn't even begin to deal with all the conflict that takes place in the workplace over credit, over money, over differing personality types and communication styles. Leaders have to make efficient decisions that affect other people and the bottom line of a business, put out fires, keep the company and team moving onward and upward, and keep a steady head. No pressure, right? We've got this!

In addition to surrounding yourself with wise leaders like coaches and peers, wisdom in the workplace comes from marrying the knowledge you have acquired with prior experience. One way to gain prior experience is to listen to your team. As a leader, you're not just responsible for yourself, nor are you always able to make decisions single-handedly. Your team is a wonderful resource because they are your boots on the ground. The decisions you make can directly affect them and their well-being. A wise leader wants to keep her team happy so that they are motivated to do their best work. Sometimes that includes listening to your team's observations, ideas, and concerns, and figuring out where you can implement their feedback to make things run more efficiently. Not every idea will be gold, but you never know where that one nugget will come from that could bring innovation to a department and make it more productive.

Wisdom in the workplace can also come from surrounding yourself with people who think differently than you. God created us as diverse, unique beings with different backgrounds, experiences, skills, interests, and strengths so we could come together and collaborate. Let's be real. How boring would it be if we all thought and acted the same way? Paul wrote, "What then is the conclusion, brothers? Whenever you come together, each one has a psalm, a teaching, a revelation, another language, or an interpretation. All things must be done for edification" (1 Corinthians 14:26 HCSB).

> Wisdom in the workplace can also come from surrounding yourself with people who think differently than you.

God made us for different purposes, and when we come together valuing our differences, it not only edifies and glorifies God, but it can also increase individual and collective wisdom. We each have things we can teach and learn from each other to build knowledge and wisdom.

I am blessed that I lead a diverse team. It makes me a better leader. Even when we don't always see eye-to-eye on things, I do my best to listen, consider, and value the input from others knowing that they might have experience in something where I am lacking or ignorant. If I am predisposed to judgment or look for people who simply reinforce what I already know, I am stagnating myself and my team. There is no opportunity to grow.

A team full of yes-men and yes-women is a danger. I want people to challenge me like the Bible says: "Iron sharpens iron, and one man sharpens another" (Proverbs 27:17 HCSB). I am sharpened by people who push me to forgo my judgments and preconceived ideas, open my mind to new ideas, and implement wisdom in finding the best path forward. In the popular TV show *Ted Lasso*, the titular character has a saying that I absolutely love: "Be curious, not judgmental."[51] That is a golden nugget of wisdom that could be considered a concise, updated twist on Paul's words about unity yet diversity in the body. Paul wrote,

> The body is not one part but many. If the foot should say, "Because I'm not a hand, I don't belong to the body," in spite of this it still belongs to the body. And if the ear should say, "Because I'm not an eye, I don't belong to the body," in spite of this it still belongs to the body. If the whole body were an eye, where would the hearing be? If the whole body were an ear, where would the sense of smell be? But now God has placed each one of the parts in one body just as He wanted. And if they were all the same part, where would the body be? Now there are many parts, yet one body. (1 Corinthians 12:14–20 HCSB)

The body is made up of diverse parts doing different tasks, all contributing to the whole. Similarly, we as humans are all part of the body of Christ. This passage of Scripture goes on to ask what would happen if the parts of the body all began judging each other instead of seeing how they work together to make something beautiful.

This is another example of wisdom we can apply to our workplace. Instead of only hiring people who make us comfortable, sometimes the best candidate for the job may be someone who, at first glance, is quite different. If we look again at the *Ted Lasso* quote, we can conclude that curiosity is a form of humility that seeks to learn from others. Judgment is a form of pride that closes us off to learning opportunities. I want to encourage you to embrace an environment with a diversity of ideas, backgrounds, politics, viewpoints, skill sets, interests, strengths, education—all these things that contribute to the complex functions of a healthy body or a healthy team.

A third area where we can apply wisdom in the workplace is risk assessment. Risk is part of doing business. We all know the saying, "No risk, no reward"; however, there is a difference between foolish risks and calculated risks. Wisdom goes a long way in making educated, calculated risks by considering the following questions:

- What are the best- and worst-case scenarios?
- What is the likelihood of the best- or worst-case scenario occurring?
- How will this positively or negatively affect my team in the short-term and long-term?
- How will this positively or negatively affect my company in the short-term and long-term?
- Who will be helped by this and how many will that be? Who will be hurt by this and how many will that be?
- Is there data to support a positive outcome based on performance history and market trends?
- Is this the best time to take this risk, or should I wait?

The answers to these questions are not always black-and-white. Even with all the proper research and all the data predicting positive outcomes, there are always unexpected things that happen. Taking risks is never foolproof even when you can take all precautions; that's why they are called risks. But the above questions utilize a type of wisdom that is often referred to as doing one's due diligence. Due diligence uses both knowledge and wisdom to consider the potential extreme outcomes and expect that the actual results will be somewhere in the middle.

Usually no decision is all good or all bad. There are pros and cons to everything. However, when you're a leader, you can't just think about how a decision will affect you. You have to consider how it will affect your team as well as your company's reputation and productivity.

In 1985, The Coca-Cola Company took a major risk in changing its classic Coca-Cola formula with "new Coke." The change sparked a massive backlash from die-hard Coca-Cola fans who demanded that the original recipe be reinstated. Within seventy-nine days, the public outcry and plummeting sales caused Coca-Cola to pull new Coke from the market and resume production of its classic Coke.[52] The company lost $30 million in product it could not sell, not including the millions they probably spent on developing the new recipe, redesigning the packaging, and manufacturing and distributing it, only to have the expense of then reverting everything back to the way it was.[53]

But Coca-Cola did not just randomly decide to replace their successful product with a "rebrand" on a whim. They first tested thousands of different recipes on large focus groups to try to find the formula that would beat rival Pepsi, but the risk still failed.[54] While the company lost tens of millions of dollars, the failure of new Coke did not bankrupt the company or cause mass layoffs. The company was able to take a step back, correct its course, and get back on track. Why? Because I would assume, though I could be wrong, that for a corporation as large as Coca-Cola, there were brains who had predicted the worst possible outcome. I would also assume that, while the data showed the probability of a worst-case scenario was low enough to take the risk, they had a plan in place to revert to what they knew worked if new Coke backfired.

Regardless, if you have a business that is working and you're considering the risk of taking it in a radically different direction, do your due diligence to see if you, your team, and your company can survive the worst-case scenario. It's great to be optimistic for the best possible outcome, and we will talk more about optimism in chapter 14, but there is wisdom and protection in due diligence.

In addition, wisdom is knowing your comfort zone with risk. Some people are natural risk-takers while others are naturally risk-averse.

Some people don't mind leaping into the unknown while others prefer doing extensive research, analysis, and forecasting. The problem with taking a leap is that sometimes there is no safety net to catch you. But the issue with being too cautious is that you can find yourself in "analysis paralysis," where you become too afraid to do anything. Eventually you have to take action.

> Wisdom is knowing your comfort zone with risk.

However, because our earthly wisdom has limitations and is finite, spiritual wisdom brings God into the situation and invites his supernatural wisdom to work. That type of wisdom is called *discernment*.

Some people refer to discernment as the "gut feeling" you get about something. A prompting or leading that you can't explain. Christians know that the "gut feeling" is actually a God feeling. It is the type of wisdom described by Paul to the Philippians, "The peace of God, which surpasses every thought, will guard your hearts and minds in Christ Jesus" (4:7 HCSB). The gut feeling is the Holy Spirit who either brings a warning to stop and reroute or a peace to move forward. There is no concrete rhyme or reason behind the feeling but at the same time, there is an undeniable sense, a leading, on what to do.

Merriam-Webster defines discernment as "the quality of being able to grasp and comprehend what is obscure." I love this definition because from a spiritual viewpoint, that clarity can be attributed to divine inspiration. That is why we are unable to fully grasp or articulate it in the moment, even though we feel it with such assuredness. It is wisdom gifted to us from the Holy Spirit that we could not otherwise have.

The Bible tells us about the different gifts of the Holy Spirit, describing it as "distinguishing between spirits" (1 Corinthians 12:10 HCSB). Although God does gift certain people with discernment just as he gifts others with the ability to prophesy, speak in tongues, or heal, I believe that any believer can have discernment. I believe that even unbelievers can have the gift of discernment even though they don't know to attribute it to God. They misinterpret it as a gut instinct, but discernment is a kind gift of God, just as he provides rain and sun to everyone on earth (Matthew 5:45). Christians, though, who are filled with the Holy Spirit, can pray for discernment the way that Solomon prayed for wisdom, and God will help them become more attuned to his leading.

When I became CEO of a surgical hospital in Louisiana, I prayed daily for wisdom and discernment because I felt like I had no idea what I was doing (shh…that'll be our little secret). I had been CEO of different companies in the real estate world, and I had built a successful business coaching firm, but stepping into the leadership role of a hospital was a whole different ballpark. I struggled daily with impostor syndrome. It made zero sense for the executive team to respect me coming into this position or trust me to make big decisions, so I relied heavily on spiritual discernment and the wisdom of the people around me to help me responsibly steer the hospital back on course.

I used every ounce of knowledge, wisdom, and discernment I had during my year in that role before God moved me back into real estate, but I managed to complete my objective to make the hospital profitable once more after it had gone through a tough season. Even though I might not have had the field-specific experience to run a hospital, I was surrounded by a team of people who did. I listened to what my team had to say, I asked good questions, and I listened. I approached things with humility and curiosity instead of judgment, fully willing to admit that I was not the smartest person in the room—or even in the building. I studied up on the latest data and performance numbers, I attended conferences and meetings, and I got coaching to help me become more knowledgeable in this new field.

What I did not recognize initially was that when they hired me, the hospital saw that I had a diverse skill set and background that they needed. They didn't need another hospital administrator; they needed someone who could cut budgets, restructure, fire and hire new personnel, all to get the company back in the black. That was tremendous wisdom on their part. They trusted that I could educate myself and rely on the team around me to get up to speed and let my iron sharpen their iron.

Now I do not say all this to toot my own horn. That is not my intention whatsoever. I share this story to illustrate that God gave me wisdom and discernment when I needed it. He equipped me for a role that was a huge risk for me to take. Just when I was finally getting comfortable there, he moved me on to a new company, where I had to rely on that wisdom and discernment once again. I clung to the words of wisdom God gave Solomon in Proverbs and prayed for wisdom every day when I felt like I was in over my head.

Wisdom doesn't make you foolproof, and discernment doesn't safeguard against every potential failure. Just look at Solomon. For being the wisest man to ever live, he still made some really large-scale bad decisions, but God honored his heart's desire to be wise and protected Solomon even when he failed. Proverbs reminds us that God is in control and uses every opportunity according to his will, not ours. Even when things don't turn out the way we plan, or things seem like a new Coke-level failure, we can use it as a learning experience as we pick ourselves up and fail forward.

So do your due diligence, learn to recognize wisdom, *pray* for wisdom, listen for the Holy Spirit's voice of discernment, and be willing to risk.

11

Stone 9: Leaders Model Integrity

Let's talk about integrity. You might be tempted to think, *Come on, Dawn, why are we talking about this? This is an easy one. Next.*

If this is a stone you're considering skipping over, wait! You might think integrity needs no further explanation, but it is a concept we constantly underestimate and needlessly overcomplicate. Wisdom goes hand in hand with integrity, yet if we don't live with integrity, we may suffer dire consequences. In its purest essence, integrity is knowing the difference between right and wrong and choosing to do what is right even when nobody's looking.

Okay, I'll give it to you. It does sound rather self-explanatory, but where leaders get into trouble is when we give in to a little temptation and then make excuses in an attempt to justify our actions. Nobody starts off embezzling millions of dollars. You don't wake up in the morning and commit Enron-level fraud. That degree of compromised integrity starts much *much* smaller, with the itty-bitty things we think are no big deal. Things like charging that small personal item to your business card. *Oh, it's just a small amount compared to what the company rakes in. They won't mind just this once. I'm a little short on funds this month. It's not that big a deal in the grand scheme of things. Other people probably do it all the time.*

Whether we are consciously aware of it or not, our pride can lead us to believe we are justified in compromising our integrity in a seemingly small matter, but then once we make one compromise, our pride will convince us it's okay to keep doing it. These small tests, when we give in to them, can become easier to repeat, easier to justify, and easier to scale. Before you know it, those small excuses and compromises in integrity snowball into bigger and more serious compromises.

I'm not trying to be an alarmist or scare anyone, but the Bible tells us that the devil knows our weaknesses: "Be serious! Be alert! Your adversary the Devil is prowling around like a roaring lion, looking for anyone he can devour" (1 Peter 5:8 HCSB). The devil doesn't want us to accomplish our why. He is a crafty adversary and he studies us. He knows that you might not be tempted to charge personal items to the business credit card, but what about taking workplace supplies home or having an extended lunch? Or lying to your boss and blaming a coworker for a mistake you made so you don't get in trouble? We have to hold ourselves to high moral and professional standards so that when we become stressed, burned out, or tired, we are not prone to giving in to temptations.

Do I have your attention now?

Integrity might not be as simple an issue as you first thought, right? There's a common saying that warns, "Don't let your gift take you where your character can't sustain you." How many celebrities have faced public humiliation because their talent took them where their character and integrity could not sustain them? Jesus told us, "Everyone to whom much is given, from him much will be required; and to whom much has been committed, of him they will ask the more" (Luke 12:48 NKJV). If we want to become more influential leaders capable of handling bigger responsibilities and shepherding more followers, we need to prioritize maintaining integrity.

Stepping Stone: Maintain Integrity Through Boundaries

We compromise our integrity when we compromise our boundaries. You say yes to too many things, get too far out of your own lane into someone else's, or try to carry too much on your own shoulders without enlisting help when you need it. One way to maintain integrity is by setting healthy boundaries and knowing your own weaknesses. Knowing where your temptations lie can help you pray for strength in those areas and build those muscles before you need to use them. Boundaries put a healthy framework in place to protect you from unnecessary stress. They set lines you will not cross.

> We compromise our integrity when we compromise our boundaries.

So often women feel pressured to say yes in the workplace to prove they belong, they are committed, and they are willing to be a team player. Plus historically, women have had to carry a lot more to earn the same respect as their male counterparts. We have had to juggle career *and* family, work *and* home. If we picked career over family, society labeled us as selfish and ambitious. Then came the pressure of being a have-and-do-it-all *supermom*. You know: the woman who always looks amazing, shows up to every practice and game, bakes everything from scratch for the school bake sale, has time for cooking meals, keeps her home showcase clean, helps kids with homework, has time for her husband, and still has time and energy to climb the corporate ladder without complaining or asking for help.

Again, this is not a slight against men but rather an acknowledgment that there are very real double standards that women still face in the workplace. They are unrealistic, cause undue stress, and feed into a false narrative that women have to grin and bear it quietly so as not to rock the boat.

Especially for younger women who are working their way up the ladder and gaining their confidence in the workplace, it can be difficult to put boundaries in place and feel like you have the right to enforce them when higher-ups ask you to go above and beyond. No one wants to be labeled as "high maintenance" or develop a reputation for being difficult to work with. Whether consciously or subconsciously, bosses can ask women to move their boundary lines.

This is not just an entirely gender-specific issue even though it is heavily skewed toward women because women generally want to people-please more than men. We care about the way others perceive us and want to be accepted into our workplace community more than men do. As we grow older and wiser with experience, it becomes easier to hold our boundary lines, but it is hard for women just starting out to feel like they have the right to advocate for themselves.

First of all, you do! Second of all, it is better to start advocating for yourself while you're young so you can build your reputation as someone trustworthy. This will also help you discipline your integrity so that as you are promoted and given more responsibility, you have the integrity to sustain you when those boundaries get tested…and they will.

There's also the unhealthy concept commonly touted in the workplace that if you want to get something done, find a busy person. It's kind of a backhanded compliment because it recognizes busy people for their efficiency and competency, but also takes advantage of dumping tasks on them since they can feel the pressure to overwork themselves in order to sustain that reputation of dependability. As a result, that person can feel overworked, underappreciated, and can become burned out. It is easy to see those healthy boundaries of integrity slip when burnout hits. You can become more tempted to grumble and complain about your boss or your coworkers, become passive aggressive in communication, and make the mistake of saying something that could get you in trouble or fired. Learning to place healthy boundaries for yourself helps prevent those overwhelming feelings of burnout.

When I was first hired as the regional director of Keller Williams Realty International's Southeast Region, their largest and number one performing real estate market, I came into the position with some boundaries that were important to my mental health. I was traveling back and forth from my home in southeast Louisiana to Atlanta every week. I would fly home on a Friday, spend the weekend with my family, and fly back to Atlanta on Sunday night so I could be at the office for Monday morning. I wanted my daughter to be able to graduate high school in Louisiana without transferring during her senior year, and I knew commuting like this would be a short-term sacrifice I would have to make. I was up front with my boss about needing this schedule, and they were more than happy to accommodate. I also told them that I would not be on call during those weekends with my family unless it was an emergency. Again, they were willing to accommodate. However, on my first weekend home with my family, they started emailing me.

I could have answered the emails and silently resented them for ignoring my boundary and communicating with me after promising not to. I could have given in and worked during the precious and limited time with my family so as not to disappoint my new employers. Instead, I responded to their email and asked if the matter at hand could wait until Monday when I was back in the office. I respectfully upheld my boundary, and they quickly apologized and told me that the issue could absolutely wait until Monday to be resolved.

By sticking to my boundary when it was first challenged, I reinforced the standard that both sides had agreed upon in our negotiation. I had been transparent in the negotiations that this was one of my no-compromise issues, and when they tested it, I did not cave. I did not become upset or rude. I reminded them of the line I had drawn, and they backed off. Boundaries are always going to be tested. Integrity means remaining firm in your boundaries.

Most of the time, when boundaries are tested, it is in non-harmful matters like this, where a simple reminder will do the trick. But sometimes, your boundaries will be blatantly tested, and you may be pushed to do things that make you uncomfortable, are unethical, or even illegal.

Your employer may even threaten your job security to try to get you to cave. Here is where you have to be strong in your convictions and say no even if it does cost you your job. It is so much better to be temporarily jobless with a clean conscience and record than to start going down a road that could permanently tarnish your reputation. Using wisdom and discernment as we talked about in the last chapter can help you find that courage of conviction in these circumstances.

I was once put in a position where a company I worked for was doing some creative accounting. At the end of each year, the executive leader knew that the numbers would look better and make him look like a stronger leader if we "cooked the books." Now, this leader was a very charismatic person, very persuasive, and he tried to encourage us to do highly unethical things, but I told him that I would not play along. I can remember this leader calling me and yelling at me over the phone, threatening to fire me.

This was a boundary moment that challenged my integrity. I needed this job. I had worked really hard to achieve the position I was in. But I had that Holy Spirit "gut feeling" telling me that this was not right. I was reminded of what God said in Proverbs 10:9, "Whoever walks in integrity walks securely, but he who makes his ways crooked will be found out" (ESV). I had to make the difficult decision of telling my leader that if he wanted me to cook the books, he could go ahead and fire me. I refused to compromise my integrity and the integrity of the company I worked for. Thankfully, my local team backed me up and stood behind me in their refusal to bend to his bullying and intimidation tactics. Months later, when the higher-ups found out what this person was doing, he got fired instead of me.

Stepping Stone: Integrity Is Modeled at the Top

A reputation can take a lifetime to build and mere moments to destroy. "A good name is to be chosen over great wealth; favor is better than silver and gold" (Proverbs 22:1 HCSB). As a leader, your integrity builds trust between you, your team, your customers, and your clients. Integrity and leadership come from the top and are modeled throughout a company. Where leaders and companies get into trouble is when they focus on profits and performance over people, place goals over methods, and overpromise but underdeliver. When results at all costs becomes the culture of a workplace, integrity is bound to be compromised.

Integrity starts at the top. When the leaders put healthy boundaries in place for themselves and for their teams, they set a standard for others to practice. One of the things I love most about Keller Williams Realty International is that they have created a culture of faith first, then family, then work. Former KWRI CEO Mo Anderson created this hierarchy of priorities and modeled it during her entire tenure with the company. Her legacy carries on to this day even after her retirement. Knowing the core values of the company gave me the confidence to ask for and enforce a boundary surrounding my time with my family. I knew that I was going to work for a corporation whose values echoed my own.

Knowing about a company's culture and values and how they align or differ from yours can help you know if the company is likely to respect your boundaries or challenge them. Doing your due diligence about the people at the top and learning about their reputation will tell you a lot about whether they are modeling integrity in the workplace. How do they treat their employees? Do they prioritize profit over people? Do they take responsibility for their actions, mistakes, and failures, or do they scapegoat and make their team members part of the collateral damage? Will they do the right thing when no one is looking?

Your integrity must increase as your influence and responsibility increases. With bigger stakes come bigger temptations. With greater privilege and influence comes greater responsibility. The people in your sphere of influence will look to you as an example of how they should behave. They will closely scrutinize your actions, what you say, and what you post to social media.

A 2021 article in the *Harvard Business Review* shared that 70 percent of employers look at candidates' social media feeds before hiring and 54 percent have rejected candidates after seeing what they post online.[55] I know when I'm hiring new people to my team, I will look at their social media to see if they exhibit the values and integrity of the company. Do they swear a lot in their posts? Do they put themselves in situations that look potentially compromising?

The Bible says, "Abstain from all appearance of evil" (1 Thessalonians 5:22 KJV). Note that it doesn't merely warn to abstain from what *is* evil. It warns to abstain even from what *appears* or can be *misconstrued* as evil. Even something that might be harmless in reality can give the wrong impression and cause an employer to question your integrity. With social media, not only is everything instantly shareable, but it is permanent, even if you try to delete it. Hold yourself to a higher standard of integrity if you want to have the moral compass to sustain a higher degree of leadership responsibility.

> Hold yourself to a higher standard of integrity if you want to have the moral compass to sustain a higher degree of leadership responsibility.

If you have any questions about integrity in a specific situation, a good litmus test is to look to God's Word. That is where you find the ultimate standard for integrity. If you question what to do or how to react to something, ask what the Bible says to do. Consult the book of Proverbs for wisdom. Google what God says about a topic. Consult wise counselors. All of these tools help strengthen your integrity so you don't make foolish decisions that can harm your reputation. If you have to question what the right decision is, odds are that you already know the answer. Do the right thing even when no one is looking.

Stone 10: Leaders Live Kindness (Part 1)

It still amazes me that kindness is one stone I have to talk about. This is the stone that should really be a no-brainer.

#IYKYK, as the millennials say.

Or as Gen Z says, "You know when something's sus."

Leaders should be kind. It's that simple. Period. The end.

13

Stone 10: Leaders Live Kindness (Part 2)

Okay, if we really need to discuss kindness further, there's no better place to look than at Jesus. Jesus was divine kindness, compassion, and love personified. He didn't just teach kindness, he lived it. He fed the needy, he clothed the poor, he healed the sick, he called the children to him, he ate with the lepers and social outcasts, he sacrificed everything so we could be forgiven. That is what I call fierce kindness. It is radical. It is extreme.

> Jesus was divine kindness, compassion, and love personified. He didn't just teach kindness, he lived it.

We've talked at length about taking the extremism out of a variety of different topics to make them more attainable, like discipline and health, but I believe kindness is the one stone, other than generosity, where being extreme can be a good thing. Extreme kindness and extreme generosity, which we will talk about in chapter 16, are doubly impactful: the more we live them out, the more they enrich not only the lives of others but also our own. It's paradoxical.

Kindness can be used synonymously with "being nice," but there is an important distinction to make between these two terms. A nice person is polite and agreeable, even kind to a degree. But the overall tone of niceness is surface-level and performative. Kindness is more genuine. It comes from a place of humility and integrity. Kindness comes from the deeper, inherent nature of a person who focuses on others above self and is ready to help.

The Bible does not talk about *nice*, but it says a lot about kindness. Paul included kindness among the fruits of the spirit that we are encouraged to embody as Christians: "The fruit of the Spirit is love, joy, peace, longsuffering, kindness, goodness, faithfulness, gentleness, self-control. Against such there is no law" (Galatians 5:22–23 NKJV). In his letter to the Colossians, Paul prompted us to put on kindness as the elect, or leaders, of God: "As the elect of God, holy and beloved, put on tender mercies, kindness, humility, meekness, longsuffering" (3:12 NKJV).

Niceness can be faked. We've all encountered people who can deliver veiled insults with nice words and a smile, but their mannerism and tone make it clear that their heart motive is not pure. Kindness is genuine. It cannot be faked because it is who you are at your core. Great leaders are kind. Kindness draws people to follow them. It inspires loyalty because it makes your team feel valued. Unfortunately, kindness is one of those concepts that can be challenging in the workplace, especially for women, because it can be viewed as weakness.

Stepping Stone: Why Kindness Can Be a Challenge for Women in the Workplace

I have repeatedly been told by male bosses that I am too kind or that I lead too much with my heart. Let me clarify that they did not mean this as a complement. What they were implying in these scenarios was that I needed to be more aggressive, more abrupt, more ruthless. When I was brand new to the corporate world, it devastated me that my kindness was being viewed as a liability, like maybe I was too soft to be in business. I only lasted three years in pharmaceutical sales because I just could not take the cutthroat nature of that industry.

Even in one of my CEO tenures, the president of the company I worked for took me aside and told me to be more of a bulldog. He was threatened that I was undermining his power with kindness and didn't like that the department heads were coming to me to discuss problems rather than going to him. By this point in my career, I was comfortable enough to not bow to his pressure. I know firsthand how difficult it can be to be kind as a woman in business or leadership, but I have also seen that kindness draws people to you. It makes them want to work with you, and ultimately it produces good results.

As women, our kindness can be misconstrued as meekness or passivity. Men can be kind but still look authoritative in their stature and vocal tone, the nonverbals we discussed in chapter 8. With our softer voices, nurturing side, and ability to empathize with others, women can struggle balancing kindness with garnering respect in the workplace. Women who are demonstrative in their body language and whose vocal tones modulate when engaging and empathizing with others can be perceived as unfirm or wavering. However, women who consciously and purposefully tailor their communication skills in the workplace for a more blunt, assertive, commanding approach can be labeled as a "witch with a capital B."

It might be tempting to look at this as one of those "damned if you do, damned if you don't" scenarios, but I believe kindness wins every single time. Proverbs 21:21 tells us that "Whoever pursues righteousness and kindness will find life, righteousness, and honor" (ESV). Proverbs is our book of wisdom and our code of conduct for acting with integrity. If Solomon tells us that being kind comes with life, righteousness, and honor, I'm not going to question God's promises. We just have to learn, as women, how to practice what I call *fierce kindness*.

When I say fierce kindness, I'm not talking about ferocity or aggression. I'm talking about *intense* kindness that comes from a place of confidence, poise, and grace. There's a degree of quiet authority and presence in the way you treat those around you and make them feel valued. Like all the other Stones we've discussed, kindness is a learned skill that you can practice. We will dig into the nuances of fierce kindness in a little bit, but first I want to discuss how science has once again caught up with the wisdom of the Bible regarding kindness in the workplace.

> When I say fierce kindness, I'm not talking about ferocity or aggression. I'm talking about *intense* kindness that comes from a place of confidence, poise, and grace.

If you're Gen X like I am, you're probably more familiar with the ideology that leaders have to claw their way to the top, that success comes from survival of the fittest and showing no mercy. There was a radical fallacy that leaders have to be cutthroat because "nice people finish last." The implication was that kindness shows weakness and a lack of drive. Workplaces became hostile and competitive environments, especially for women. Women had to affect a hardness of demeanor to command respect, and they had to fight for limited positions of leadership. The Gen X businesswoman had a ruthless quality that partly stemmed from the 1960's second-wave feminism and partly from a rejection of the nurturing domestic housewife. It also resulted from the inordinate amount of value placed on competition in the workplace.

The women who shattered the glass ceiling to make way for the rest of us had to overcome insurmountable obstacles. They had to rely heavily on grit and determination, but they also had to sharpen their claws and compromise kindness and integrity to prove they belonged with men in leadership roles. But again, I don't want to dwell on the past problems. I want to steer you toward the future.

Thankfully, the culture of the workplace began to recognize how toxic an environment that level of competition created for its employees.

Many companies have switched their cultural philosophies to reflect what studies are showing about the impact and importance of kindness, things that the Bible said over two thousand years ago.

An article by *Psychology Today* shows that "it takes strength and power to be truly kind."[56] A study by *Harvard Business Review* states that when kindness is modeled in the workplace, it creates a more positive work environment: "If you're an emerging leader, being kind to your employees can help you retain top talent, establish a thriving culture, increase employee engagement, and enhance productivity."[57] Sounds a lot like what Solomon told us in Proverbs!

The Mayo Clinic published an article online about how kindness can be catching. They refer to it as a "spirit" that can sweep through the workplace. The effects boost the mental health of team members.[58] I don't doubt this for a second because kindness undermines the selfishness of competition and self-centeredness to get ahead at all costs. Not to say that there isn't healthy competition or fun competition. A little interdepartmental rivalry can lead departments to bond and strengthen team spirit. But I have never liked the idea of individualism over teamwork in the workplace. Perhaps it comes from playing high school sports and learning early in life that "there's no 'I' in 'team.'" When one person tried to steal the spotlight, the team suffered in comparison to when we came together and were able to share our wins and losses as equal peers.

Kindness can boost serotonin and dopamine and decrease cortisol, the stress hormone.[59] In the health chapter, we discussed how these hormones impact mental health. Kindness is an intentional act that releases good hormones while suppressing bad hormones. It makes you feel good when you are kind. It also builds trust with your team.

Beyond the obvious that kindness draws people to you and makes them feel comfortable sharing with you, it also builds trust because people remember how you made them feel far longer and deeper than they remember what you said. When you make your team members feel secure in knowing that you genuinely care about their welfare as people rather than performers, they will naturally want to perform better for you. They know you will have their backs and that you celebrate their wins. Kindness fosters a spirit of unity. We are stronger together than we are alone. You as a leader can have that effect by modeling kindness from the top and watching how it catches like wildfire.

Another fallacy about kindness in the workplace that is starting to change with current research is the misconception that showing kindness means you are a pushover or can be easily taken advantage of. Here is where having those firm boundaries can easily help shift the narrative. Kindness does not always mean telling everybody else yes; clearly communicated boundaries are a good way to say no to others kindly. As women, we want to help each other. We're empaths and social beings. We value community and feel good about ourselves when we are able to help others. It is easy to see where women can be viewed as pushovers when they say yes to too much and become overwhelmed. Plus, the workplace is one of those environments where you can be easily taken advantage of when you prove yourself to be hardworking and efficient. Putting those boundaries in place and learning how to say no with kindness and firmness is a crucial skill.

Women can also struggle with kindness in the workplace when correcting a team member. Nobody likes to do it, but as a leader, you will have to. Just as parents learn to correct their children in love, leaders must sometimes correct their team to uphold the standards of the workplace. It doesn't feel good, but it's another skill to practice. Men can sometimes be too blunt and overlook the fact that women are deep feelers and emotional beings. Women can either be too severe in an attempt to show their power and authority or they can be too wishy-washy out of fear of losing respect or relationship. There is a balance that we can achieve with practice, where we deliver correction with firm kindness. Kindness does not mean letting mistakes slide; it means extending mercy and using the situation to point out learning opportunities so that the same mistakes are not made again.

> Kindness does not mean letting mistakes slide; it means extending mercy and using the situation to point out learning opportunities so that the same mistakes are not made again.

Correcting in kindness can look like using constructive criticism rather than tearing someone down, or it can mean having those difficult conversations, like we discussed in chapter 8, and asking how you can win or lose with a team member. It's treating others with dignity and respect even when it may be difficult. You can be kind even when firing someone! How's that for a radical concept? If you've ever been fired, you know it can feel like one of those humiliating rock-bottom moments of failure. It can feel even worse if your boss is yelling at you or making you feel even smaller than you already might feel. Firing people doesn't feel much better for the person doing the firing. I've been on both sides and can speak from experience. I do not enjoy firing anyone.

The very first time I had to fire someone was when I was running Mochaccinos. I had to fire one of my baristas. I was in a season of overwork, I had just opened my second location, and the stress of overseeing two locations was getting to me. I had a worker who was not a good employee. He was not very teachable and needed to move on to something new. He wasn't happy in his position anymore, and his attitude and performance reflected it, but I was still so upset. It was terrible. I could barely get out the words, "You're fired." I did not handle it well at all. I may have been more upset than he was!

Thankfully he found a new position and went on to get married and have a beautiful family, and we are still friends on social media. However, I look back and cringe at how I fired him because I never would have wanted somebody to fire me that way. I have since learned how to fire someone without breaking into tears, but I really try to avoid firing someone at all unless I have caught them doing something illegal or highly unethical. Instead, I try to coach someone up or coach them on to a new position.

I just had a team member who was not right for the position they had been hired for. This person was talented and hardworking but not performing well in their current role. Instead of calling them into my office and firing them, I had one of those difficult conversations. The reality of the situation was that this person didn't belong in my department, but they had a number of skills that would have benefited a different department. I told this person that I recognized the ways in which they were an asset to the company, but that I thought they might perform better in a different role. When I pointed out what I saw, this person agreed with me and was willing to let me coach them into a position they were better suited for. In this instance, the person was able to successfully transition to the other department and remain on our staff. That is an example of coaching someone up.

In other cases where a person really isn't working out in their position and there is no other place where they can move, I will try to coach that person on to their next opportunity. I will try to find out what that person is good at and encourage them to use those skills to find a job that they can shine in. It is still never easy, and it hurts to be let go, but I have heard from several people whom I have coached on who later thanked me for being kind enough to make them see that their gifts were better suited in a different place. Some of these people went on to other corporate positions where they are thriving or even went into business for themselves.

When you can, have the difficult conversation and ask, "What's next for you?" Sometimes the person will already suspect they are not in the best position for their personality or talents, and by having this conversation, you can help them relocate within the company or remind them of the tools they have to change lanes. Coach them up or coach them on, and do it with kindness.

I've already shared that people remember how you made them feel longer than they remember what you said. Jesus was the ultimate example of correcting in kindness. Look at how he handled the situation with the woman at the well. Jesus pointed out the fact that the Samaritan woman had committed the sin of adultery: "Jesus said to her, 'Go, call your husband, and come here.' The woman answered him, 'I have no husband.' Jesus said to her, 'You are right in saying, "I have no husband"; for you have had five husbands, and the one you now have is not your husband. What you have said is true'" (John 4:16–18 ESV). He didn't point out her flaws to condemn her, but to convict her in love. It was only after Jesus showed the woman her sins and she humbly accepted the responsibility for them that Jesus offered the gift of forgiveness and eternal life.

We should follow Jesus' example in giving correction and having difficult conversations as leaders. We do not have to tolerate poor performance or excuses in the workplace, but we as women, as leaders, as Christians, do have the responsibility of treating people with kindness and respect. Sometimes those conversations will restore and strengthen relationships, other times, relationships will still have to be terminated, but you can navigate it from a place of fierce kindness.

Stepping Stone: Practicing Fierce Kindness

Let's talk about how we can practice fierce kindness in the workplace. I make this distinction because we cannot be the same type of *kind* at work that we are with our family and friends. With friends and family we can relate with greater transparency and unguardedness. In the workplace, part of reinforcing your power, authority, and position while maintaining kindness comes from establishing a degree of professional distance from your team. That can be hard for women.

Have you ever heard the saying, "It's lonely at the top"? Women can struggle with this. We want community. We want to build relationships in our networks, but to be a leader does mean you have to practice being friendly without necessarily befriending the members of your team. Men are much better at this than women. First of all, men do not crave community as much as women do, and second, they are better at establishing relational boundaries in the workplace to protect their authority. It is harder to respect someone and follow someone whom you feel equal to. Let that sink in for a second.

Women leaders can also struggle with kindness in the workplace when they are too concerned with being liked. You may want to be friends with the people on your team, but to lead, there must be a degree of separation so they will respect your position. Think about the difference in how you relate to your friends versus how you relate to your parents. With your friends, there is a close connection that comes from viewing yourself on an equal plane with them. With parents, there is often a respect for their authority as the people who raised you that creates a degree of distance no matter how close you may be with them.

The same dynamics apply in the workplace and, for women in particular, maintaining that distance requires exercising self-control. You cannot have your team approaching you with the same familiarity as they would when they approach a friend. It becomes too easy for them to lose respect or potentially undermine you, even if it's unintentional, when you ask them to do something. You have to be more like a parent to your team, which means establishing boundaries. These can be tricky waters to navigate, but it is doable.

Another way I try to practice kindness in the workplace is by celebrating my team. I encourage my team with words of affirmation, not just when they are performing well but also when they are struggling. A little encouragement can go a long way in helping your team over those difficult hurdles. It can give them a little boost, a reminder to keep going, that they've got this. From time to time, I will also take my team to lunch or treat everyone to a special coffee break. We always keep a pot of coffee brewed in our office break room, but every now and again I will run to the nearby Starbucks and surprise my team with a treat. We will use the time to fellowship and collaborate, to team build, and to give me the chance to check in with them. I use the spontaneous coffee break to show them that I observe the hard work they are putting in and want to give them uninterrupted time to voice their concerns while I listen to the challenges they may be unsure how to face.

> I encourage my team with words of affirmation, not just when they are performing well but also when they are struggling.

I try to ask open-ended questions to facilitate sharing and collaborative problem-solving. Leaders ask good questions and teach people how to think, right? I use this quality time to listen and brainstorm with them, offering guidance when needed, to keep us all moving forward together. I genuinely care about my team. A team lunch or impromptu coffee break is a small yet meaningful way to remind them I am there for them.

If you are from the Southern US and have ever road tripped with your family, Buc-ee's is a must-stop destination. It is like Chuck E. Cheese, Cracker Barrel, Walmart, and the world's largest (and cleanest!) gas station all wrapped up into one. Their mascot is a beaver that is featured on every possible kind of merchandise. People often do Christmas shopping for the whole family at Buc-ee's—that's how large and iconic a place it is. There are countless YouTube videos dedicated to people's first experiences with Buc-ee's, and they're hilarious to watch. Every time we would take a road trip with the kids, we made a point to stop at Buc-ee's.

I have a coworker who is obsessed with Buc-ee's and always made a point of stopping at one when she went on road trips. Every year she tried to get the special, limited-edition Buc-ee's holiday shirt. That's how much she loved Buc-ee's. One day, during the holiday season, when Manly and I were driving home from a business trip in Huntsville, Alabama, we passed a Buc-ee's. We immediately thought of this coworker and decided to stop so we could surprise her with a holiday shirt. It was literally a split-second decision, and we really didn't think much of it. It was just something we did just because we thought it would make her smile. In fact, we were so excited to give it to her that I didn't want to wait until Monday morning at the office, so we surprised her at her house.

When we gave her that shirt, you'd have thought we had given her a million bucks. She was so touched by that small act of kindness. She thanked me in person, texted me later on to thank me, and then gave me a hand-written thank you note at the office which blessed *me*! It was so neat to see how that little gesture not only provided us with a way to show her kindness but also prompted her to reciprocate with kindness as well, in a way that impacted me back. I am a sucker for a hand-written thank you note. Not enough people do that these days.

Buying the T-shirt was one of those acts of kindness simply meant to bless my coworker. There were no strings attached. I didn't want anything in return. I wasn't trying to manipulate or buy her loyalty, and she realized the motive behind the gift was genuine and heartfelt. Kindness cannot be faked.

Kindness may seem like a simple concept, and it is, but there are some nuances to practicing kindness as female leaders in the workplace. It takes so little effort to be genuinely kind. Kindness comes from a place of authenticity compared to being nice, which people can fake. However, kindness does not mean you have to always say yes or come across as weak or a pushover.

You can practice fierce kindness in the workplace by setting healthy boundaries. Boundaries actually make it easier to be kind because they will keep you from taking on too much and becoming stressed or short with your team. Boundaries will build trust and loyalty between you and your team, increase team unity and performance, and boost your mental health. However, there is a level of intention and discipline in practicing fierce kindness because you have to maintain professional distance and protect the respect between a leader and her team.

As a leader, think of the difference between how you relate to your friends and how you relate with your parents. You must enforce a degree of separation from your team so they respect you and don't unintentionally or intentionally undermine your position. This does not mean you have to be arrogant or witchy with a capital B. You can be kind and respectful when correcting and having difficult conversations with your team.

A kind word or gesture can go a long way to showing your team you are paying attention to their efforts and have their back to lead them through difficult times. You don't have to shy away from confrontation or correction but can correct in kindness just like Jesus did. Ultimately, it takes some practice but it really does boil down to five simple words: be kind to each other.

Stone 11: Leaders Choose Optimism

Kindness was an easy concept to talk about. I believe deep down, we all strive to be kind. Optimism, however, is one of those concepts people routinely challenge me on, usually people who are prone to negativity. I'll admit, it's much easier to be a pessimist and keep your eyes focused on the dirt rather than up toward the mountaintop, but great leaders have learned that optimism is a trait worth having.

But Dawn, you just don't understand the life I grew up in. Optimism is a result of having privilege. Let me remind you, I grew up below the poverty line. In a trailer park. Surrounded by addiction, abuse, disability, and chaos. Life was never easy. There were many times when I was tempted to give in to the reality of my circumstances and I wondered if I could ever make something of myself and get out of the trailer park.

Growing up in the trailer park, there was nothing but despair. It's hard to have optimism when you're struggling to put food on the table and help your mom pay the electric bill. Every day was a struggle. But I *chose* to be optimistic. I saw it modeled to me by teachers and by people I met in church, and I observed that the people who practiced optimism seemed to attract good things. Like a magnet, they drew people and opportunities to them. While living in the trailer park, I learned to practice optimism day in and day out with the belief that I could also attract good things. If I can do it, you can certainly do it too.

Optimism is a state of mind, a choice, an inclination. It does not come naturally. Being an optimist means believing that there is better to come than what your current circumstances tell you. Does that sound familiar? To me it sounds a lot like what Hebrews 1:1 tells us about faith: "Now faith is the reality of what is hoped for, the proof of what is not seen" (Hebrews 11:1 HCSB). It takes faith to have optimism. My husband, Manly, refers to optimism as "faith with a capital O." I want to equip you with some stepping stones you can use to grow in optimism in your life as a leader. And not just optimism, but extreme optimism.

> Optimism is a state of mind, a choice, an inclination.

Stepping Stone: Optimists Expect Good

When I talk about extreme optimism, I want to clarify that I am not talking about unrealistic or ignorant optimism. Extreme optimism does not turn a blind eye to problems or believe that you will never go through trials and tribulations. These are going to be part of life on this earth. You can't avoid reality, but you can choose to frame it through a positive and expectant lens.

I like to practice extreme *practical* optimism. This may sound like an oxymoron, but stay with me. Imagine you're on a boat that springs a leak. Unrealistic optimism would tell you that if you just believed hard enough and tried not to focus on the problem, the boat won't sink. Or worse, the boat will miraculously fix itself. That's not extreme optimism. That's stupidity. Extreme *practical* optimism acknowledges that the boat is sinking but chooses to believe you'll survive because you have options. You could tread water or float until another boat comes along, or you could swim to shore. You could fix the leak or at least slow it to buy time. You have practical options you can choose from to remind yourself that the sinking ship will not sink *you* even if the waves around you seem scary.

During the 2008 financial crisis, when so many real estate jobs were on the line due to the housing market collapse, it would have been easy to look at the circumstances and become overwhelmed. None of us knew if we would still have jobs in a month, or even a week. It was a volatile situation, and as a leader, I was the one my colleagues were looking to for guidance and reassurance. I knew they were depending on my attitude and outlook to gauge morale.

I'll be honest, I was scared just like the other members of my team. I had never lived through a recession of this magnitude. I was still relatively new to the real estate field, and my colleagues were looking to me for answers. I had to choose to be optimistic. That didn't mean that I ignored the crisis and pretended it wasn't happening, but I did my best to validate the concerns of my colleagues and put on a brave face in the midst of them. Their concerns about their careers and livelihoods were legitimate. We had many difficult conversations in which I acknowledged that none of us had control over the grand scheme of things. We couldn't predict what would happen with the market, but we could control what we did for the next twenty-four hours, and the twenty-four hours after that, and each subsequent twenty-four-hour span.

We came up with daily, weekly, and monthly growth plans. We set goals with the mindset that we would make it through this storm. We might have some cuts and bruises along the way, but we would survive. We banded together to encourage each other about what we could control versus what we couldn't. It helped us unite as a team, and when we had small victories, we celebrated them as if they were major victories.

Even in the midst of a global recession, we managed to perform above expectations because we used extreme practical optimism. We didn't expect the hardship to magically go away overnight, but we chose not to let the hardship paralyze us with fear or keep us from moving onward and upward.

When I became the Gulf States regional director of Keller Williams Realty International, I was thrown into my new position in the midst of a literal storm. My start date with the company was August 1, 2020, and on August 27, the Category 4 Hurricane Laura devastated Louisiana with winds of 150 miles per hour at landfall. I was in North Georgia closing on the sale of our family cabin, and I had to rush to the nearest office supply store to print out the Keller Williams manual for disaster relief because it was part of my job to lead disaster relief efforts for our KW associates and their families.

I can remember sitting in my hotel room and poring over that thick disaster relief manual, trying to absorb everything as quickly as possible. I had never done anything like this before, especially of this size and magnitude. Sure, I had lived through Hurricanes Katrina and Rita and many other hurricanes over my lifetime, but now I was in a position where I had to lead a relief effort and encourage our team members, many of whom had just lost everything they owned and probably felt like they were still drowning even though the storm had passed.

When I arrived back in Louisiana and was driving through those coastal towns that had sustained the worst damage, it was hard to be optimistic. People were standing on empty slabs where their houses had once stood. Entire structures had been uprooted by the winds and waves. There were boats and cars in the trees. Personal belongings were scattered like damp confetti in the streets.

People were sifting through the damage for anything they could salvage, basic items like clothing and sentimental items like family photos. They were dealing with the physical and emotional impact of losing everything they had worked so hard for, the lives they had built, the places where they had raised their families. People were crying, and it was my job to give them some comfort and assurance that we would all be okay. And I had only been on the job for a few weeks. I felt scared and completely underprepared. Let me tell you, if you've never lived through a major natural disaster, it's overwhelming physically, mentally, and emotionally.

Thank God, I had already been working on these twelve stones and practicing them for a long time. I could rely on the discipline of my leadership training to kick in and keep my emotions between the lines. Even though I had not been directly affected by this particular storm, I knew firsthand what it was like, having lived through others. I was able to use wisdom from personal experience to moderate how I communicated optimism and hope.

The last thing I wanted to do was to be a toxic optimist and negate the reality of the crisis at hand, but I also knew these people needed hope in addition to the practical things I was bringing in, like generators, bottled water, flashlights, and food. I took time to talk with these families, listen to them, cry with them, and pray with them. I reminded them how we had rebuilt together through the Katrinas and the Ritas even though the evidence of the current disaster really made me question if it was possible to do it again. However, I had disciplined myself in optimism long enough to know to "fake it till I make it." I knew that as a leader, I could not show up to the front lines exuding the fear I felt inside.

> I had disciplined myself in optimism long enough to know to "fake it till I make it." I knew that as a leader, I could not show up to the front lines exuding the fear I felt inside.

Generals do not show up to battle looking scared. They may be frightened between their ears and fighting pessimism, but they put on an optimistic face for their soldiers. They keep their men and women believing victory is near.

After a few days, I could see the fighting spirit coming back to people. I could see the optimism of myself and the numerous first responders, other volunteers, and relief aid organizations taking root. My faith and optimism became more grounded as well. I no longer felt like I was just going through the motions because it was a strength I had built through discipline for moments like these. Now it was starting to feel organic. We navigated the immediate aftermath of a major disaster together.

You want to know what happened next? It happened again. Just over two weeks later, Hurricane Sally hit. Then another hurricane, and another hurricane. Five hurricanes hit in a row that summer, and I had to visit each and every one of those devastated communities, bringing supplies and hope. I lived in my car for several months. With each hurricane, it was easier to have optimism and share it with others. I knew that we had the resources and tools to bring relief, and I learned that the areas we visited were not going to stay devastated forever. I knew that we would get through the initial devastation and help the community get back on its feet to start the long rebuilding process because I had lived through it time and time again.

I used what I learned to rewrite our company's disaster relief policies, and optimism was one of the principles I included because I saw it in action. I helped share the message that recovery and rebuilding would be difficult, but we would be okay. We were going to expect it and manifest it together.

Stepping Stone: Optimists Look for Reasons to Celebrate

Another part of being an optimist is not only expecting good outcomes but also choosing to celebrate the wins. This might seem like another one of those "duh" moments we probably don't need to spend a lot of time talking about, but it is far too easy to overlook the small victories in everyday life. Once more, it is a choice. Where are we going to put our focus? It can be easy to focus on the negative, the shortcomings, and how far we have to go. However, it is more productive to focus on the positive.

Let me reemphasize, this doesn't mean discounting reality or turning a blind eye to areas where growth is necessary, but it is choosing not to dwell there long-term. By finding reasons to celebrate your victories and your team's victories, you are focusing everyone's attention on the positive.

There is tremendous research showing the importance of positive psychology. Modern science is now proving things that the Bible has told us to do for ages. One of those areas is deciding how to think. Positivity and optimism are just as catching and contagious as negativity and pessimism. Where do you want your focus and your team's focus to be? Paul tells us, "Set your minds on what is above, not on what is on the earth" (Colossians 3:2 HCSB), and 1 Corinthians 15:33 says, "Do not be deceived: 'Bad company corrupts good morals'" (HCSB).

> Positivity and optimism are just as catching and contagious as negativity and pessimism.

While we may interpret the Colossians verse to mean placing our minds on the eternal and not being tempted to consider life on this earth as our ultimate home, another interpretation can apply to being optimistic. When we focus our minds on what is above, we are choosing to look above and beyond our present circumstances. Paul warned of the consequences of pessimism or "bad company." He said that these can corrupt our morals, or integrity, and what's worse, it can spread to others and corrupt their outlook as well. Proverbs 17:22 puts it a different way: "A cheerful disposition is good for your health; gloom and doom leave you bone-tired" (MSG). I don't know about you, but I don't want to be bone-tired. That's pretty serious!

Modern psychology is finding that optimism is good not only for your mental health, but can do wonders for your physical health too, supporting what the Bible says. Optimism can reduce depression and anxiety, decrease stress, boost heart-health, and prevent premature death.[60] In a study on the progression of atherosclerosis in middle-aged women, researchers found that women who were optimistic thinkers rather than pessimistic thinkers slowed the effects of the hardening of their carotid arteries post-menopause.[61] In a separate study on optimism and women with breast cancer, pessimism shortened predicted life expectancy and increased the risk of premature death compared to women with breast cancer who remained optimistic during their treatment.[62]

The women in both of these studies who chose optimism and celebrated the small victories in the midst of their health struggles had real, quantifiable results that showed the healing impact that positive thoughts and actions can have on their bodies. Talk about an incentive for us, particularly as women, to choose positivity! I want to embody that positivity and share it with everyone I can.

Let's apply this to the workplace. When you celebrate the victories, I don't mean that you have to throw a huge party for each win that you have. What I am saying is that you make the conscious decision not to let these winning moments go unnoticed. These are milestones that you and your team are accomplishing together. Nothing makes your team feel prouder than when you, as their leader, acknowledge and celebrate the results of their efforts. Going back to our parenting analogy from the last chapter, how good does it feel to celebrate a good report card with your child? You can see how your child's face lights up when you tell them, "Good job!" Just those two words can boost their self-confidence, increase their self-esteem, and make them believe they can keep doing better.

> Nothing makes your team feel prouder than when you, as their leader, acknowledge and celebrate the results of their efforts.

Similarly, celebrating the victories as a leader in the workplace doesn't have to be an overly demonstrative or extravagant display. It can be as simple as sending an email to a team member to tell them that they did a good job handling a difficult client. It demonstrates that you are paying attention, you are acknowledging what you have observed, and most importantly, you are choosing to go the extra step to celebrate them. It's an extension of kindness that makes a deliberate decision to focus on the positive while spreading it to your team. We've already talked about how optimism is contagious, right? Celebrating your team's victories is a subliminal way to spread optimism. They don't realize that when you choose to celebrate them, you are building their trust, building their esteem, and making them believe they can keep excelling.

Your praise and belief in them in turn helps them believe they can go further than they originally thought. Furthermore, that belief will spread to other members of the team. When they see you celebrating one member's victories, it makes them feel secure knowing that you will take the time to celebrate them as well. That optimism and the desire to be celebrated will spread through your team.

But we also know that leadership is modeled from the top down. If you are modeling negativity and pessimism, that will translate to your team. The tone of your workplace is never net-neutral. You are always either moving 1 percent forward or 1 percent backward. You can choose where to steer your team. Will you steer them with optimism or with pessimism?

Scientific study supports this "emotional contagion" model that Paul stated, "Do not be deceived: 'Bad company corrupts good morals'" (1 Corinthians 15:33 HCSB). Emotional contagion does not just apply to emotions like sadness, fear, anger, or happiness. It can also apply to psychological mindsets like optimism and pessimism. Even small nonverbal actions like smiling versus frowning can shift the mood of those around you, and we, as women, are predisposed to being highly attuned to nonverbal communication. If you walk around the office all day stressed out and with a scowl on your face, you will be less approachable and more intimidating to your team. If you have a peaceful and content demeanor and your facial expressions reflect that, it will also translate to your team.

I'm sure you've heard about or maybe even know someone who "lights up a room"; that is the contagious effect that optimists have. They exude it, and it's unmistakable.

Your team is constantly watching you, as their leader, and discerning the nuances of your nonverbal communication to tell them if you are optimistic or pessimistic about the work environment. I can guarantee you that if you lean into negativity and the temptation to let real-world scenarios scare you, your team will feel that. That fear will translate to them and directly affect their performance. Your productivity will decrease because your team won't believe that *you* believe their efforts will make a difference. If you lead your team with optimism in the face of adversity, your team will follow your lead, and productivity will increase. If you go the extra step to celebrate the good with them, your team will follow you into any battle, no matter how hard, because they know you will lead them to victory.

Stepping Stone: Optimists Look for Memorial Stones

The last piece of extreme practical optimism I want to discuss is looking for the memorial stones in your life. We've talked about expecting the good and celebrating the small victories. Searching for memorial stones is taking a moment every now and again to look back and appreciate how far you've come. When you look back and reflect on how much you've overcome, it reinvigorates you to keep moving forward during times when you are weary.

> Searching for memorial stones is taking a moment every now and again to look back and appreciate how far you've come.

I am such a believer in the principle of memorial stones. It's the name, logo, and concept for 12 Stones, my coaching and consulting business. As I explained in the introduction, when I was in the trailer park seeking solitude in the woods from the violent chaos of my everyday life, I would look for interesting stones to collect and mark my walking path.

Even before I became a Christian and learned the significance of memorial stones, I had spent my life looking for them. As a child, they were real stones that lined the path I trod in the woods looking for peace from a violent and chaotic household. As an adult, the stones became more metaphorical and symbolic, reminding me of what I came from and how far I've come physically, practically, and spiritually. On days when I'm tempted to get down on myself for not being where I want to be, those memorial stones remind me of all the progress I've made. They commemorate some of the biggest adversities I've overcome and wins that I've celebrated, and they inspire me to keep going.

As I write this book, I have started picking up physical stones again from my travels to serve as tangible memorial stones of how God is working in my life. For example, I just got back from speaking in Cape Town, South Africa, and I took a stone from the winery where we did our first service for the church we planted there. I brought that stone all the way back to Atlanta with me not only to remind me of that church but also to commemorate my first international speaking opportunity—something that has always been a dream of mine. Not bad for a girl from the trailer park!

As I've shared before, the twelve-stone monument from Joshua 4 is the basis for this memorial habit. The monument the Israelites built was to serve as a reminder of God's deliverance of the Israelites from slavery and captivity. From protecting them from the plagues delivered in Egypt on the first Passover to leading them out of Egypt and parting the Red Sea, from feeding them as they wandered in the desert for forty years to delivering them to the promised land, from giving them the Ten Commandments and the ark of the covenant to establishing them as God's chosen nation, the twelve stones signified every time God had fought on Israel's behalf. They were a physical testament that they could look at to remind themselves of God's goodness as he fulfilled his promises to them even when they doubted. We are to do the same.

I look back on my life and see all the times God saved me and delivered me. I should not be where I am today. There is no reason I should ever have gotten out of the trailer park or broken free from the trailer park mentality that keeps so many stagnant in poverty because they don't know anything different. I look back and see how God saved my life by taking my dad's at such an early age. If my dad hadn't been paralyzed, I believe he eventually would have killed us all in his anger and depressed state. He had certainly threatened to do so many times. I can remember after the stroke that partially paralyzed my dad, he still would try to physically hurt me as I took care of him. But he was in such a weakened state that he couldn't inflict the damage he intended. I believe God, in his mercy, took my dad to spare the lives of me, my mom, and my siblings because he had a greater purpose for us.

I look back at how I stepped out and opened Mochaccinos and built it from nothing into seven successful locations. No experience, virtually no money—nothing but a vision to have a coffee shop that would glorify God and be a place where people could gather and fellowship. God blessed me in my ignorance and made up for my weaknesses as I underwent some massive growing pains, but I'll never forget how my mom came to me toward the end of her life and asked me if she could have her own Mochaccinos franchise.

My mom had gotten pregnant with me so young that she had to drop out of school. She had never gotten to pursue her hopes and dreams. She worked so hard to keep a roof over our heads and put food on the table. I didn't even know until she asked me that she always had a desire to own her own business. By this point, she was well into her battle with breast cancer. I tried to talk her out of it, but she was adamant. She wanted to have something at least once in her life that she could call her own and be proud of. I'll never forget the look on her face when she opened her franchise location. It was an unforgettable moment shared between a mother and daughter. A memorial stone of what we had been through together.

There are so many memorial stones that I can look back on to strengthen my faith and optimism, moments that remind me that if God helped me to overcome *that*, he is more than able to help me overcome whatever is facing me at the present moment. Start looking for those memorial stones in your own life and building your monument today. Write them down and put them where you can pull them out to meditate on when you need to encourage yourself. They will shift your focus from the ground back up to the mountaintop. They will help you look beyond the waves and give you the motivation to step out of the boat.

Memorial stones will keep you moving in optimism. As a leader, you get to decide to be optimistic. You get to make the choice to expect good things, look for reasons to celebrate, and mark those moments with memorial stones. You have an opportunity to influence your team's productivity with extreme practical optimism and to model it in everyday life. Choose to live with optimism.

Stone 12: Leaders Have Faith

As Christians, we've frequently heard the Hebrews 11:1 definition of faith: "Faith is the substance of things hoped for, the evidence of things not seen" (NKJV). Another translation says, "Faith is the reality of what is hoped for, the proof of what is not seen" (HCSB). I like that translation better because it feels more concrete, but I prefer to think of faith as believing in something bigger than yourself. When I think of faith in this manner, it reminds me that I don't have to be in control of everything.

I think it's easy for women to feel like we have to be in control of everything: our homes, our marriages, our kids, our work. As someone who had to assume way more responsibility than any kid should have when I was young, I definitely felt the pressure to be in control. It turned me into an overachieving, high-performing perfectionist. It made me successful, but it made me anxious for years because I wrongly assumed I had to do it all on my own.

Faith introduced me to the all-powerful Creator whom I could trust to fill in the gaps when I failed. Not only that, I could go to God personally and ask him for help. It removed the pressure of feeling like I had to keep all the plates spinning like a circus performer. We weren't designed to do everything in our own strength. We were designed to need a God. More specifically, we were designed to need a Savior.

Faith also gives us a purpose bigger than ourselves. It shifts our minds to the eternal. When it is easy to focus on self and become myopic, faith reminds us that this earth is not our home. This life is like a school that prepares us for our greater eternal purpose. Yes, we have a purpose and a why here on earth, but we also have an even bigger purpose for when we get to heaven. We are building God's kingdom here on earth. That is our ultimate why.

> We are building God's kingdom here on earth. That is our ultimate why.

I shared with you that God revealed to me that my personal why was to become a servant leader, to lead by being the hands and feet of Christ so my leadership would hopefully point people to God. We all have an eternal home, and we get to choose where we want to spend it. Faith in God and the invitation of the Holy Spirit into your life purchases your eternal real estate in heaven using the blood of Christ. Knowing that helps me step back and take a look at the big picture when life on earth gets hard and I'm tempted to quit.

There's a verse I often hear misquoted and misinterpreted. People think the Bible says that "God won't give us more than we can handle," and they will say that to comfort themselves when life starts to get overwhelming. The verse people think they're referring to is 1 Corinthians 10:13. What it actually says, and I like *The Message* translation of this, is "No test or temptation that comes your way is beyond the course of what others have had to face. All you need to remember is that God will never let you down; he'll never let you be pushed past your limit; he'll always be there to help you come through it" (MSG). The crux of 1 Corinthians 10:13 is that God will not let you be pushed past your breaking point. That doesn't mean he won't push you *to* your breaking point.

We will all be led to our breaking point at some time in our lives. Your breaking point is where faith begins, when you come to the end of yourself, and you *have to* call on someone stronger than yourself to pull you back out of that pain cave. First Corinthians 10:13 promises that in that moment, God will never let you down.

Faith is the structural cornerstone on which all the other stones frame your temple for success. Without faith, you can practice all the other stones to build your house of leadership and influence, but it will not be safe when the storms of life hit. Just like when I was doing disaster relief after Hurricane Laura and saw the homes that had been separated from their foundation, your house can be completely shaken and moved off course without faith.

> Faith is the structural cornerstone on which all the other stones frame your temple for success.

Paul said in 1 Corinthians 3:11, "No one can lay any other foundation than what has been laid down. That foundation is Jesus Christ" (HCSB). There is nothing else in this world that will be a stronger cornerstone than Jesus Christ.

When Peter discerned that Jesus was the true Messiah, Jesus told him, "Blessed are you, Simon Bar-Jonah, for flesh and blood has not revealed this to you, but My Father who is in heaven. And I also say to you that you are Peter, and on this rock I will build My church, and the gates of Hades shall not prevail against it. And I will give you the keys of the kingdom of heaven, and whatever you bind on earth will be bound in heaven, and whatever you loose on earth will be loosed in heaven" (Matthew 16:17–19 NKJV). Not only does faith create a cornerstone that not even the gates of hell can prevail against, but it also gives you a direct connection to the spirit world. We are given the authority as Christians to access eternal influence by binding and loosing things in the heavenly realm. We don't have to wait until we get to heaven to enjoy some of that spiritual power to fight the enemy and unleash the blessings of God here on earth. That should help give you some confidence to hand the reins of control over to God.

I'll never forget the time God showed up for me in the rock bottom of my pain cave and exponentially grew my faith. I'll preface first that I had had a relationship with God since I first set foot in a Catholic church just down the corner from the trailer park I lived in. I was a kid playing outside by myself, and I saw all these other people going into the church. Not knowing any better, I followed them inside wanting to see where they were all going. From the moment I first entered the building, I felt this overwhelming peace. It was unlike anything I had ever experienced in my life of constant loud, noisy, and violent chaos. I was addicted to that feeling. I made a point to start going to church by myself every Sunday until I graduated high school and moved away to college.

Then I got busy.

Even though my dorm was right next door to another Catholic church and I spent a lot of late nights studying in the church, my relationship with God fell away due to busyness. I didn't have the same commitment that I did as a kid. When my first husband and I got married and began having kids, we started going to a nondenominational Bible church and got very involved there. I began building a relationship with God, but this time, I became very legalistic in my faith. I got really good at using the Bible to pass judgment on others instead of showing mercy.

Then my marriage fell apart. As if that weren't enough, most of our church friends sided with my ex-husband, and I felt abandoned by my church family. I literally felt like I was dying. I was so alone and just trying to keep my head above water as a newly single mom. Then my mom's cancer came back.

I remember crying out to God so many times, telling him that I couldn't handle any more. I was trying to do it all in my own strength, being a single working mom who was still homeschooling three young children. I was depressed, I was anxious, I was stressed beyond belief and completely depleted. Our finances were a mess, and my health was also suffering. It got to the point where I had lost too much weight and my hair started falling out. My ex-husband took me aside one day and told me he was worried about how gaunt I looked. We were barely even speaking at that point. It was a wake-up call. I had nothing left. I was at my breaking point. I had to let go of control and learn to trust God.

It's funny looking back how the one of the worst days of my life was also one of the highest points in my life because of how God showed up so miraculously. My mom was on her deathbed. She had been fighting cancer for so long that she no longer had the strength to keep fighting. She was in so much pain, and she was fearful. Even angry. Even though she was a believer, the cancer had spread throughout her body and brain so that she turned from an incredibly loving person to someone who was uncharacteristically mean. It was killing me to watch the cancer slowly take her like that.

She had wanted to die at home, but it got to the point where she was in such agony that I literally picked her up, physically put her in my car, and drove her to the hospital. We got to the emergency room, and I told the doctors that I knew she was dying. We didn't need help saving her, but she needed morphine so that she could pass in peace. However, my mom was highly allergic to morphine. I can remember my sister, my brother, my stepdad, and me arguing in the hospital because they knew that as soon as they gave her the morphine, her kidneys would fail because that's how allergic she was to it. The doctor finally helped convince them that Mom only had a few hours left and that she deserved to die without pain. We all watched as they put the morphine into her IV, and immediately, she had peace. My aunt and uncle arrived, and we had just enough time to say our goodbyes.

I held her hand, and as I did, I told her that I forgave her for everything. I knew she was out of it and that she couldn't hear me, but I felt her spirit pass out of her body and literally move through my hand to my arm to my chest and across to my other arm and hand as she went to heaven. There was a palpable shift in the room that everyone felt. It was the most intense peace I had ever felt in my life. In that moment, I felt all the shackles—everything I had been struggling with: the trauma, the pain, the lingering unforgiveness, the mental and emotional abuse—break.

God let me feel my mother's spirit pass into his loving arms from her body, and instead of loss, I received a healing that surpassed understanding. It was such a powerful moment for me. It proved without a shadow of a doubt that God is real, and he loves me. He didn't have to give me that, but he knew I was at the end of myself. He knew this was what I needed to bolster my faith and keep going. There have been so many other times in my life when God has showed up for me, but this was that pinnacle, life-changing moment when I surrendered control and let faith take over.

Every single person's faith journey is going to look different. Your journey will not look like mine. God will meet you where he knows you are. Sometimes it will be in big moments like these when you are at the end of yourself, but a lot more often, it will be in the little moments when you get away with him one-on-one. If you're wanting to learn how to build your faith, I'm going to share with you a few things that have helped me over the years.

> Every single person's faith journey is going to look different. Your journey will not look like mine. God will meet you where he knows you are.

Stepping Stone: Faith Requires Getting Away with God

If you want to grow in faith and learn to hear God's voice more clearly, the number one way to do that is to put him first. It's literally a commandment. The *first* commandment: "You shall have no other gods before Me" (Exodus 20:3 NKJV). How many of us struggle to put God first in the midst of everything else we juggle? It can be so easy to put God off and make excuses for why we let him drop to the bottom of our priority list. I can only imagine that this has to hurt him. I know as a parent that it hurts my feelings when my kids are too busy to call or FaceTime. I want to spend that one-on-one quality time with them because I love them. They're all grown now and out of the house, and I miss them. It makes me feel loved in return when they call their momma.

How much more so must God feel this ache as our heavenly Father? He wants to spend time with us and talk with us as his kids. When my kids call, I want to hear their hearts. I want to hear what they're going through—the good, the bad, and the ugly. Plus, as a parent, I want to teach them from my experience. It makes me so happy when my kids ask for my advice. I try not to force it on them because they're adults, and as parents, we sometimes need to let our kids make their own mistakes so they can learn (that never gets easier!). However, when they invite me to share my experiences to help them avoid some future pain, *and they listen*, I'm on cloud nine. Believe me when I tell you that God wants to do this for you. You have to put him first, which means making time for him, which means—you guessed it—discipline.

If you're starting out wanting to build your faith or you're a new Christian who is unsure how to discipline yourself to make time with God, aiming to pray an hour a day is going to be unrealistic. Those read-the-Bible-in-a-year plans are wonderful, but even they can be unsustainable for some people. When I get to Leviticus or Numbers—those are dense to get through even for a Bible scholar, which I don't profess to be. They can discourage many people from finishing their Bible reading growth plan out of sheer boredom to the point where they don't want to pick up the Bible again for months or years.

I recommend starting small. After all, God honors your heart. When you begin to seek him, no matter how small, he will reward that.

My gratitude journal has helped me carve out manageable time every morning and evening to visit with God. I write down what I'm thankful for, and I thank God for those things. I pray about things that are weighing on my mind and listen for that still, small voice to give me wisdom and discernment. Sometimes I read in my Bible, but some days I read in a devotional. There are so many good devotionals to get you through a month or a year by taking a verse each day and pulling out fresh meaning and revelation.

I have disciplined myself to start and end my day focused on God and gratitude, but I also talk to him throughout the day. I'll say a short prayer in the middle of my workday if something comes up that I don't know how to handle, if something comes up that is stressful and I want to invite his peace into the situation, or when I just want to tell him thank you for something. These are all sustainable things that build my relationship with God, and I know it blesses his heart as much as it blesses mine.

Another wonderful way to grow in your faith walk, especially as a new believer, is through finding a church that feeds you. Since the COVID-19 pandemic, it's become even easier to do that without leaving your house. I don't know if that's necessarily a good thing, but it certainly gives you the ability to try new churches and find one that will help you grow through the study and application of the Word.

Even though I went to Catholic church every Sunday in junior high and high school, I didn't really consider myself a Christian until I was in college. It was February 13, 1997, and I accompanied my sister to First Baptist Church in Covington, Louisiana. During their altar call, I felt God drawing me to the front of the church. When I opened my eyes after repeating the Sinner's Prayer, I saw my sister standing next to me. She had made a profession of faith that same day. That's when I really invited Jesus into my heart and began building my foundation of faith.

It doesn't matter what denomination you are as long as you belong to a church that is Bible-based. There are too many churches that have gotten away from the Bible and become emotionally, topically, or politically led. Since relocating with my new job, it's been hard for me and Manly to find a new church family, and I miss that community. However, I have not let that stop me from reading the Bible and listening to podcasts by some of my favorite pastors or tuning in to our old church home online even though it's now several states away.

There are so many resources now to help build your faith on-the-go, way more than I had back when I was a pharmaceutical rep listening to Lifesongs Radio, the only Christian FM station, while I drove all over creation. Nowadays there are tons of messages available on YouTube, social media, podcasts, and even different apps. God can use any platform he chooses to speak to someone. He's the ultimate influencer.

> God can use any platform he chooses to speak to someone. He's the ultimate influencer.

While I have developed discipline to put God first in my daily routine, my favorite times with God—and the most powerful times I have with God—are my sabbaticals. I've mentioned sabbaticals in a few chapters, but this is where I'm really going to get into what they are and why I think they are so important.

Sabbatical comes from the word *sabbath* which, in the Bible, referred to the day of rest, according to the Jewish calendar. God put the Sabbath in place to commemorate the day when he rested after six days of creation. Talk about modeling leadership from the top! The God of the universe took a day of rest after creating the heavens, the earth, and the human race, and then made the day of rest a commandment because he knew how badly we, as humans, would need one. It's not just in the top ten; it's in the top three.

The Sabbath was supposed to be a day of rest and rejuvenation, a day to put God first. I would venture to say it's been a long time since any of us have had a proper sabbath. About twenty years ago, I began going on retreats. A lot of personal development books at the time talked about the importance of getting out of your normal routine and going away somewhere to engage in self-reflection. I began doing that several times a year, but about five years ago, I shifted my retreat into a sabbatical for spiritual growth. For me, sabbaticals are more focused on prayer and fasting than my retreats used to be. It is a time for me to get away with God and get closer to him. When I did retreats, they were focused more on me and for my benefit. Usually I was trying to accomplish something, even if it was only to relax. I was more concerned with what *I* was getting out of my retreat rather than getting away to be with God. Now I use my sabbaticals to leave the daily grind and busyness of my routine behind and to really get totally alone with God. I'm doing it *for him*, not for me. (Okay, maybe a little bit for me).

I pick a place, usually a cabin in the woods, where there is no Wi-Fi and I can be surrounded by nature. I put my phone away, take my Bible, a journal, and a pen, and spend several days alone with God in prayer and fasting. I don't watch TV, and I don't even bring other books to read because I want as few distractions as possible so I can listen for God's voice.

I'm always amazed at how God will meet me in powerful ways when I take the time to really be alone with him and put him first. It never fails that he will start giving me all these ideas during my prayer and meditation time with him. I also use the time to check in with my growth plans for the year and reflect on what is helping and what is hindering my progress in meeting those goals. I pray for God's guidance, invite him into the plans I made, and listen for where he prompts me to redirect.

There have been several times when God has redirected my plans, like when he opened the door for me to become CEO of the surgical hospital. That was not on any of my growth plans. The opportunity came to me, and I honestly didn't know what to do. It was a major career change, and I didn't think I was even qualified for the job. Any time I have that big a life decision to consider, I will take a few days and go on sabbatical. During my time away with God, he showed me a verse in the Bible and gave me a visual image that confirmed that I needed to take the job.

It was one of those discernment moments where, on paper, it didn't make sense. But when God led me to the verse in one of my daily readings and then gave me a visual to go with it, I felt that peace that surpassed understanding. Where there had been anxiety in trying to reason it out with head knowledge, God directed my steps with his wisdom, and I accepted the job.

I try to go on a sabbatical once a quarter, but at the very least twice a year. My most important sabbatical is in the fourth quarter, when I reflect on the previous year and plan for the year ahead. This is when I ask God to give me a word and a verse to hold onto for the year. For 2023, the word was *wisdom*, and the verse was Isaiah 50:4: "The Lord God has given Me the tongue of the learned, that I should know how to speak a word in season to him who is weary. He awakens Me morning by morning, He awakens My ear to hear as the learned" (NKJV). God showed me that what Isaiah 50:4 refers to as "the tongue of the learned" is another word for wisdom. He was going to use that year to help me grow in speaking wisdom to those who needed to hear it (including myself).

In addition to my personal word and my personal verse, Manly and I also ask God for a word and a verse that applies to our marriage, and one for our family. Every year, God has met us with one.

Sabbaticals have become such a crucial time for me in building my faith and my relationship with God. It is my time to unplug and rest, and I always walk away feeling rejuvenated, reinvigorated, and refocused to pursue my why. If you are not certain what your why is yet, I cannot encourage you enough to get away even for just an afternoon, put the phone on "Do not disturb," and spend several hours with God. Be sure to bring your notebook and a pen because you never know what he will share with you when you put him first.

God put you here on this planet for a purpose, for such a time as this. If you ask him to make it clear to you why that is, I guarantee you that he will reveal his purpose to you. When he does, he will make your path straight so you can build your house using the rest of these twelve stones on that solid cornerstone of faith.

Stepping Stone: Faith Leaves a Legacy

The last thing I want to say in this faith chapter is for the women who might be closer to the end of their careers or at least thinking about their retirement. Here is a question for you ladies to think about: "What is the legacy you want to leave behind?" Have you ever thought about this? You were created to leave a legacy here on earth for generations to come. Your legacy extends to your family, but as a leader, you are appointed by God to have influence beyond your family. That influence is not just for the present. It will have a lasting impact that lives beyond you. As Christians, our legacy is also a way to point people to God.

I love what the Bible says about legacy in Psalm 78:4: "We must not hide them from their children, but must tell a future generation the praises of the Lord, His might, and the wonderful works He has performed" (HCSB). If you read this chapter in conjunction with Psalm 77, you will see that this Scripture verse is the climax of the psalmist reflecting on a particularly tough period of testing. The psalm relates the trials that he was facing, but he repeatedly chose to be optimistic and have faith in God to deliver him. He looked at the memorial stones in his own life where God showed up powerfully to help him stay optimistic and full of faith. By the time we get to Psalm 78, we see the shift in the psalmist's tone. He now thinks beyond himself and starts thinking about the legacy of faith he wants to leave future generations. We are those future generations now benefiting from his wisdom.

As I am looking at the next ten years, I've been thinking a lot about my legacy and the things I need to put in place, not just physically but also spiritually, to leave a lasting impact on the world. When I look back at my life, I recognize the memorial stones that have marked just how far I have come from the trailer park where I grew up. I was the first person in my family to graduate high school, go to college and graduate, build a successful business, run a literal marathon, and then run several ultra-marathons. I did not want my kids growing up the same way I did, surrounded by poverty and addiction. I wanted to break those generational curses that had plagued my family so I could leave a powerful legacy for generations.

It took a lot of hard work, discipline, grit, and faith, but I already see the effects of the sacrifices I made. Every one of my children is either in college or has graduated from college. They have gone on to do things at their young ages that I marvel at. They are so far ahead of where I was at their age in life, in faith, and in wisdom. I hesitate to say this, and I want you to understand that I don't say this in any way out of pride or to toot my own horn but out of full knowledge that all glory and honor is due to God. But I also know that had I not worked to break those chains of poverty that were part of my legacy, it is all too probable that my kids and I would still be stuck there. They would have had far fewer opportunities and a far greater challenge to make something of themselves.

In addition to seeing my kids already living out my legacy and creating a legacy of their own, part of the legacy I still want to build revolves around sabbaticals. The dream that Manly and I share, the dream we've been working toward in our professional careers, is to be in a place where we can build a retreat center for sabbaticals. We had both long ago decided we wanted to have an active retirement doing something we loved. We wanted to build channels of passive income so we could leave our kids a nice inheritance, but we didn't know what our retirement *why* would look like. Retiring to a trailer park in an RV has zero appeal to us. To me, having grown up in that reality and seeing that the mindset of the people who do that is one of stagnation and death, I want to keep building things and growing in my retirement. One year while Manly and I were on a sabbatical, God gave us the vision to build a retreat center for sabbaticals.

Having that vision became part of our long-term growth plan. We began to prioritize health so that we could be active enough in our retirement to build and run this retreat center. We created discipline in our finances so that we can afford to buy property to develop our retreat center. Knowing how powerfully God has shown up in our sabbaticals, Manly and I want that to be the legacy we pass on to others. We want to build cabins and an event center where we can host individuals, groups, and corporate teams who wish to get away with God. We want to be able to teach and guide sabbaticals, create an atmosphere of peace, have walking trails out in nature for people to collect their own memorial stones, and build a place where other people can come discover their why just like we did.

We are hopeful that our sabbatical vision will bless the people who come to get away with God, will bless our kids with an inheritance, and perhaps encourage our kids to take it over after Manly and I are gone. It gives me goosebumps to think about. I am excited for my retirement because of the legacy I want to leave behind. Start praying today about the legacy God has for you to leave. He will show you if you get away with him.

I am so in awe of how God has worked in my life. From drawing me to him as a kid—when I didn't even understand that the peace I felt when I stepped into church for the first time was him—to seeing how he healed so much of my emotional trauma when he let me feel the passing of my mom into his loving arms at her deathbed, God has continually shown himself strong in my weakness. My faith has become rock-solid, the cornerstone on which I built my life and my influence as a leader. It has been there when I felt like second-guessing myself or when I was tempted to be driven by emotions and circumstances. My faith keeps me on track when life tries to distract me, overwhelm me, and pull me off course.

Faith has shown me my why and given me a clear vision for the legacy that I want to leave behind. It has broken chains that kept my prior generations from living their best life, and it has given my children a head start to do even bigger things. I am able to rest in God and surrender to him the need to be in control because of faith.

> Faith has shown me my why and given me a clear vision for the legacy that I want to leave behind.

I like to say that I am a woman *on* faith. A friend of mine has this hilarious T-shirt that says, "Running on Diet Coke and Dry Shampoo." I am running *on* and living *on* faith. Every day I am calling on the God of the universe to stand in the gaps where I am weak. I take such comfort in realizing I don't have to know everything or have everything figured out because I know the one who does.

I encourage you to be strong in your faith, put God first, and listen to all the amazing things he wants to share with you. Faith is the last of my twelve stones of leadership and by far the most important one.

But wait! There's more!

16

Lagniappe Stone: Leaders Give Generously

When I came up with my original twelve stones, I realized that I left out a very important one: generosity. I believe that great leaders give generously, so I decided to throw this stone in as the thirteenth stone or, as we say in Louisiana, a little "lagniappe." *Lagniappe* is a Cajun French word that means something extra, a gift. It's kind of like the extra donut thrown in to make a baker's dozen. It comes from the heart and is intrinsic to Louisiana culture. We love looking for ways to provide a little lagniappe to bless someone's day.

The Bible has much to say about the importance of heartfelt generosity and giving, although there is one type of giving for which God offers us his protection, and it is the only promise in the Bible where God asks us to test him to see how he will honor it. "'Bring the full tenth into the storehouse so that there may be food in My house. Test Me in this way,' says the Lord of Hosts. 'See if I will not open the floodgates of heaven and pour out a blessing for you without measure'" (Malachi 3:10 HCSB).

A tithe refers to a tenth, or 10 percent, of what you earn that you give back to God. Malachi writes that when you do this, God ensures that your storehouses will be protected and remain full, and that if there is any doubt about this, we should test God. Give your tithe in faith and see how he opens the floodgates of blessing. Not just monetary blessing. I have seen God do incredible things from restoring marriages, curing infertility, healing diseases—things that only God can do he *will* do because his children stepped out in faith and generosity through tithing.

Tithing and generosity are a mind shift and a heart shift that trusts God to provide. Jesus said that "no one can be a slave of two masters, since either he will hate one and love the other, or be devoted to one and despise the other. You cannot be slaves of God and of money" (Matthew 6:24 HCSB). Greed is the opposite of generosity. It closes one's heart to God and can become its own god. There are so many leaders who become preoccupied with hoarding their wealth, and while they might become richer, they become paranoid and unhappy.

> Tithing and generosity are a mind shift and a heart shift that trusts God to provide.

Make no mistake, nothing we earn or achieve on this earth is ours. It is all from God, and we cannot take it with us. There is no reason not to live generously. Not only does living generously do wonders for our mental health, but it also opens the doors for God to give us more. Generosity keeps us from walking around with clenched fists, anxiously coveting our own goods, and stressed from the fear of losing everything. Instead, it shifts our heart and mind to things above so we can walk around with our hands open instead. We can walk in peace and relief when we are generous. God gives to us, so we can give to others.

Paul said, "In every way I've shown you that by laboring like this, it is necessary to help the weak and to keep in mind the words of the Lord Jesus, for He said, 'It is more blessed to give than to receive'" (Acts 20:35 HCSB). Jesus also said, "Give, and it will be given to you; a good measure—pressed down, shaken together, and running over—will be poured into your lap. For with the measure you use, it will be measured back to you" (Luke 6:38 HCSB). Giving blesses you as much as it blesses the people you give to. It refocuses your brain from carrying the weight of protecting what God never intended for you to carry.

This is not to say we shouldn't be wise stewards, which the Bible also instructs us to be, but we cannot outgive God. He is the ultimate giver. When we put him first in our lives and place our faith in him to provide for us, he will honor that. We should be extreme givers just like we should be extreme practical optimists.

When I was growing up, I saw generosity modeled to me each and every Christmas though I didn't become aware of it until I was in junior high. It was all my family could do to afford a roof over our heads, food on the table, and electricity. With my mom being the only working parent, I've already shared how I started working in fifth grade. I did odd jobs to bring in an extra $50 per week to help make ends meet. We had no money for luxuries, only the bare necessities, but every year, we had Christmas presents.

It wasn't until I was in seventh or eighth grade that my mom admitted to me that they had never bought us a single Christmas gift. All those gifts had always come from the church. Every year, the local church adopted our family and bought Christmas presents for me and my siblings. I can remember one year I really wanted a bicycle. I thought for sure nobody would buy me a bicycle for Christmas, but that year, the church blessed me with a bike. You'd have thought someone had handed me the keys to a car. I was so excited, and I rode that bicycle all over Bush. The church modeled extreme generosity to me from a young age.

I also saw generosity modeled in my young life when I went off to college. I had gotten a scholarship to cover my tuition and housing the first year—there was no way I could have afforded to go to college otherwise—but I had no money to buy things with which to furnish my dorm. I can remember one of my high school teachers giving me a graduation gift of a hundred dollars to help me buy basic items for my dorm room, like sheets and pillowcases. That was a lot of money back in those days. I was so moved by her generosity. She was by no means making extravagant money as a teacher, but she was so proud of me and wanted to help me succeed, and she expected nothing in return. Her gift helped launch me out of the trailer park.

That's perhaps one of my favorite things about generosity and why I view it as an extension of kindness and empathy: there are no strings attached. Again, it's part of that mind shift and heart shift. You do it because you want to. You do it out of the goodness of your heart realizing that God has gifted to you everything you have, and it is part of your legacy to pass it on to others.

> That's perhaps one of my favorite things about generosity and why I view it as an extension of kindness and empathy: there are no strings attached.

I want to take some time to reframe generosity for you. We are often limited in our understanding of generosity because we think it applies only to money. Money may be something we do not have in great excess. Tithing can take great faith when you are on the brink of subsistence living. That shouldn't stop you from being generous though. While giving money is certainly one way we can be generous, it is not the only way or even the most important way.

After the 2016 floods that devastated parts of southeast Louisiana, there was a family in our community who had lost their house to the unexpected floodwaters. They had nowhere to go. They couldn't afford to rent an apartment while they waited for insurance companies to pay out the funds for them to rebuild. The house Manly and I bought had a guest house in the backyard that we offered for them to live in until they could move back into their house. Again, this is not to make you think, *Oh, aren't they such good people*. We knew our house was not our own. It was a gift from God, and we wanted to share that gift with people who needed a home. We did not expect anything in return, not rent, not even utilities.

When we bought our house, we told God that we would use it for his glory, so when he brought this family to us, we told them they could stay as long as they needed until their house was ready. We didn't even know the family when they moved in, but over the months that they stayed in our guest house, they became part of our family. Letting that family stay with us was a way that we were able to be generous with something other than money. Just as the families who adopted me and my siblings each Christmas were generous with their resources, so our house was a resource with which we could be generous.

Resources can come in endless varieties. Your home is a resource. We hosted our church small group every Thursday night for years. We started a group called Operation Teen Leadership to teach our kids and their friends some of the leadership skills I've shared with you throughout this book. It wasn't supposed to be a big thing, but the kids loved it so much that we eventually had thirty teens from around the community at our house every Sunday night for two years.

Another way we used our house as a resource was to provide a home for several foster kids that arrived on our doorstep out of the blue. Some of these kids looked like they hadn't had a real meal in days. They came to us from some of the really bad-off areas around our town, where there was a lot of instability and addiction, very much like the situations in which I had grown up. We opened our home to them and treated them like our own kids. We wanted to model a stable home environment and give them a safe place to sleep and be fed.

Food can be another resource that is easily overlooked. Manly often stops at a fast-food restaurant to pick up food to give to the homeless people he sees living in tents around the city. When I do meal prep for the month, I make a few extra meals to freeze and give away to people who are in a pinch. The church we went to in Louisiana was wonderful about coordinating a program where people could volunteer to bring meals to other church members who had recently gone through surgeries or to new moms who had just given birth. I signed up to do this so many times because it was an easy way for me to be generous. It's funny, though, because I would always make a casserole to bring, so after a while whenever my kids saw me making a casserole, they would ask who was sick or had just had a baby. Bringing food is a wonderful way in which we can be generous to help fill a need in someone else's life.

One of my favorite resources to give is books. I love giving books to people. I once bought a whole case of *The Five Minute Journal* from Intelligent Change to give to people throughout the year. It is a resource that has blessed me and been a part of my daily routine for over a decade, and it is something I love to share with others. If there is a book that I think will bless someone else like it blessed me, I will gift it. I am a huge believer that great leaders are readers, and giving books is another way to show generosity and positively impact the lives of others with knowledge. Resources like your home, a meal, or even a book can demonstrate extreme generosity without being lavish or expensive.

In addition to resources you already have at your disposal, you can be generous with your talent, your energy, your network, and your time. Extreme giving doesn't mean going into debt. It means looking for ways you can share with others anything God has given you without expecting anything in return. One year, my sister-in-law made me a memory quilt out of all the T-shirts my mom and I had collected over the years. It is one of the most special gifts I've ever received because I knew the thought and time that my sister-in-law put into making it. It didn't necessarily cost her money, but the effort she put into making it—knowing that it would be something I could look back on and fondly remember moments with my mom—touched my heart so deeply. Every time I look at that memory quilt, not only am I reminded of my mom, but I'm also reminded of my sister-in-law's extreme generosity.

Similarly, when I was a senior in high school and still living in the trailer park working three jobs to help support my family, there was no way I could afford dress shopping for my senior prom. Extreme generosity was modeled for me once again when my aunt decided to bless me and actually *made* my prom dress. She wanted me to feel special and beautiful. She didn't want me feeling left out while all my friends were shopping for new dresses. So she used her talent as a seamstress to make me a one-of-a-kind custom prom dress using extra material she had. She used her time and her talent to be extremely generous so I could feel special and included in my senior prom.

Your talent, energy, and time are all resources that don't cost money to share but can make a big impact on others. It really is the thought that counts the most with extreme generosity––letting someone know that you care enough to go out of your way, using what you already have at your disposal, to bless them. There are so many ways you can make a huge, lasting impact on others by simply giving of yourself. I love when I see videos online of people volunteering their musical talents at retirement homes. The joy that it brings to the residents is so pure. Or when someone with a particular athletic gift volunteers to coach a community sports team.

> It really is the thought that counts the most with extreme generosity—letting someone know that you care enough to go out of your way, using what you already have at your disposal, to bless them.

Volunteering is one of the easiest ways to share your talents, but another way is to become a mentor. Taking someone else under your wing, sharing your experience with them, and helping them grow in their talent is a way of being generous. If you have a gift in finance, mentor someone who needs help with their finances. That is a talent, trust me! Mentors donate their talents or skills without expecting anything in return. They want to pay it forward to the next generation.

Energy is a resource I didn't even realize was a resource until I was reading the story in Mark 2:1–12 where four men lowered their disabled friend through a roof so Jesus could heal him. When I really stopped to think about this story, I couldn't believe the effort and energy those friends exhibited. Let's just assume that the average man back in Bible times weighed about 150 pounds. Imagine carrying a 150-pound man on a cot through the streets of Capernaum. That alone is a generous and strenuous effort. Then these men hoisted their friend on top of a roof. Picture hoisting a 150-pound body up to a second story.

As if that weren't a big enough effort, they had to do some demo work. These men dug a hole big enough to fit a 150-pound man through the roof so they could lower him before Jesus. The upper body strength and endurance it took to do these things definitely required a lot of energy, yet the four men didn't expect anything in return for themselves. Their sole motivation was to see their friend healed. Those were extremely generous men. I would imagine they were sore for days after that!

Time is arguably our most precious resource because it is limited, and we have so many things competing for it, especially as women. Our kids need our time, our spouses need our time, our friends desire our time. Our jobs and households also take up a lot of time. As leaders, we also have teams and the people in our spheres of influence who need our time. However, time is the one resource that we cannot get more of. No matter how hard we try, we cannot discipline our way or growth-plan our way into getting more time. We have to learn how to prioritize our time while still being generous with it, and that is why I categorize time as the most important resource.

Not only does it cost us when we give generously of our time, but it also shows someone how important they are to us to get our undivided attention. Many of the people in my circle know how crazy my schedule is, so when they ask me if I could spare some time to have coffee with them and help mentor them to get their business over a particular hurdle, they are so grateful when I say yes. When I am generous with my time, I am telling that person, "Hey, I believe in you. You are valuable. I'm going to prioritize you."

Before our move to Atlanta, I used to give quality time to the people in my life by inviting them for front porch chats. Our house had a beautiful front porch like something out of a *Southern Living* magazine. It was a welcoming, relaxing, and safe environment, and it made people feel special to sit on the porch swing and have a cup of coffee. I would listen as they shared their heart. It made them feel like they could be vulnerable with me and risk with me. When I invited people for a front porch chat, I wanted them to feel like I wasn't going to rush them. When people start sharing their heart, the last thing you want to do as a leader, or even as a friend or mentor, is to rush that. People crave quality time. There were so many times when I didn't even need to say anything in return. I just needed to listen and give someone a hug to encourage them.

When you are generous with your time, your talents, your energy, your money, and your resources, you are being obedient to God and helping to build his church here on earth. Generosity keeps your heart pure and shows your faith in God to provide for you. When you hold your resources too closely, you turn them into an idol that will only bring anxiety as you try in your own power to protect them. As with the lagniappe illustration, choosing to be generous helps us spread joy and kindness to others, and it is the one area where God encourages us to test him and see if he doesn't multiply back to us what we give.

Everything you have is a gift from God, including every breath you take. Great leaders look for ways to be generous and model generosity to others by living their lives with extreme generosity. Look for ways you can honor God and live generously.

> Everything you have is a gift from God, including every breath you take. Great leaders look for ways to be generous and model generosity to others by living their lives with extreme generosity.

Conclusion

Final Thoughts from a Trailer Park CEO

It's approaching dusk, and Manly and I are out for one of our evening walks. The sky is filled with the brilliant colors of another beautiful sunset and the fireflies are starting to twinkle along the path. We pass a fountain near one of the historic buildings close to where we live. It is surrounded by these incredible red stones into which the water has etched lines and jagged edges along its path. I am suddenly transported back to the woods where I grew up, a young girl seeking solace in nature, picking up interesting rocks and pebbles along the way to line my trails.

I pull into my office in the morning and see more stones lining the common spaces around the monolithic skyrises. These stones are much grander and made of heavy black granite. Like everything else in the office park, no expense was spared. Not even on the decorative stones. I am struck by the realization that stones have always played such an important part in my life. Before I even knew the biblical significance of memorial stones, I was looking for them, collecting them, and using them to build a legacy. As I grew, the stones in my life became more impressive, maturing with me from season to season.

The young girl I was then could never have foreseen how God would use those stones to build a life of influence, to have a platform to train up a new generation of women leaders, to encourage you who are now reading this book—the fruition of all those stones—that you, too, can arrive into achievement and have a mighty impact on those around you. If you Google meaningful statistics about the upward mobility of children who grew up in trailer parks, you won't find much even though an estimated twenty million Americans, or 6 percent of the population, still live in trailer homes.[63] And the studies you *can* find do not show favorable outcomes.

In an essay entitled "The Social Wasteland: America's Trailer Parks," the author writes, "Trailer parks in America exist on a strange axis. They share many of the same 'issues' that inner city communities face, but lack the same level of public scrutiny." The statistics of children who make it out of that life to create a better one paint a bleak picture. In a study by the US Department of Agriculture of ten teens who grew up in a trailer park, "two flourished while growing up in the trailer park...four teens were identified as static, likely to attain the economic status of their parents. And four were floundering, heading toward narrowed life chances." To this day, the majority of trailer park residents still live below the poverty line and depend on government welfare programs to provide basic needs. There remains so much addiction, domestic violence, abuse, and instability in some of these communities. The same is true of many families who experience intergenerational poverty where children grow up in conditions of poverty, continue their adult lives living below the poverty line, and raise their children in socioeconomic situations similar to the way they were raised.

You don't just get to walk out of the trailer park or out of poverty. It is often an intergenerational self-perpetuating cycle that is incredibly difficult to break for numerous reasons, but even more so for women than men according to a 2024 study by the National Academy of Sciences, Engineering, and Medicine. The study states that men have more opportunities for upward mobility than women, but even among both sexes, it is still statistically difficult to break generational poverty when it is what you have grown up in and been exposed to as normal.[64] It takes an undeniable amount of vision for a better life, perseverance, and discipline. You have to grit your teeth and fight your way out. But you don't have to battle alone. God is right there with you. He will help you achieve victory. You don't just get to walk out of the trailer park. You have to grit your teeth and fight your way out. But you don't have to battle alone. God is right there with you. He will help you achieve victory.

> You don't have to battle alone. God is right there with you. He will help you achieve victory.

Why am I telling you this? Because there is no reason why I should have ever made it out of the trailer park. There was nothing special about me compared to the other twenty million Americans who shared the same background. But for God. If God could use me, taking me out of a trailer park in the nowhere town of Bush, Louisiana, and bringing me up to the C-Suite of a Fortune-500 real estate firm, I *guarantee* you that he can do the same with you because he is no respecter of persons. There is no excuse why these stones that I have applied in my daily life can't also apply to you. It's time to stop making excuses and begin stepping into your why.

I never expected to go into real estate. I thought I wanted to go into medicine, but God had other plans that he revealed to me when I spent quiet time getting away with him. As I moved into the path God was laying at my feet, bit by bit, he enlarged my vision and my territory both as a businesswoman and as a leader. However, it all started with making choices. In choosing to make daily changes to the way I thought, the way I conducted myself, and the way I disciplined myself in the small things, God began blessing me with greater and greater responsibility because he knew I could handle it. He can do it with you too.

I wish I had had a book like this when I was first starting out in my professional life. I wish I had written this book a decade ago so my kids, especially my girls, could have had it to set them up for success when they were first starting out in life. These stones are such important tools to have in your tool kit as a godly businesswoman looking to navigate your way through a secular man's world.

However, having read these twelve—well, actually thirteen—stones, I know you might be feeling a little overwhelmed. You might have reached the understanding that success is simple but it's not easy. However, nothing worth achieving in life is easy. The things we work the hardest for are the things we hold most dear because we know the effort and sacrifices we made to get there. We have earned each stone we add to the monument we will leave behind to inspire the generations to come.

This book was designed to give you a diverse tool kit so you can fulfill your purpose and accomplish your why. It is the labor of a lifetime of practicing discipline and grit, of failing forward and choosing to pick myself up, dust myself off, and remain optimistic and faith filled. It comes from having surrounded myself with people who held me accountable and helped me grow in wisdom and integrity. It is the result of the labor of writing down the vision and working each and every day to move 1 percent closer to my goals. Of learning to communicate effectively and show that kindness is not weakness but the embodiment of reflecting Christ's love in action. Of realizing that I cannot take our health for granted, and I must learn to be generous with my time and resources.

I have gritted my way through life's storms—not just the hurricanes and floods I've lived through but also the years of poverty, abuse, and depression. I have cried out to God to give me his strength to keep putting one foot in front of the other when I was deep in the pain cave. When my mind, body, and emotions were screaming at me to quit and give up, I dug down deep into the reserves of perseverance and resilience I had built up because I had seen it modeled where I lived.

I thank God that he raised me in southeast Louisiana, where I was surrounded by people who were used to "hunkering down," as we commonly say, riding out the storms, and rebuilding together. We may get knocked down from time to time, but we refuse to stay down. I learned to put on my big girl pants, brush myself off, and push through difficult seasons, knowing that a better season was around the corner if I didn't stop moving.

If you're going through the darkness of your own pain cave and your senses and emotions are playing tricks on you, trying to pull you off course, keep putting one foot in front of the other. You are closer to the finish line than you realize, and that glorious sunrise is coming. When Thomas Edison was working to invent the light bulb, the adage goes that he failed ninety-nine times before he finally found success. We don't really know how many iterations of the light bulb Edison went through before he found the one model that worked. He could have let all those failures discourage him, make him doubt his skills and falsely label himself rather than separating his failures from who he was as an inventor. Instead, the story says that when asked about his failures, Edison merely explained that he didn't view his failures as non-successes. He just chose to reframe them as learning opportunities. He had discovered ninety-nine ways not to make a light bulb. Talk about learning to fail forward and remain optimistic.

I look back at the failures in my own life and wish I could have handled them with as much poise and confidence as Edison. As humans, we will fail, but instead of letting that define us as individuals, we must reframe our failures as learning opportunities. Especially as a woman and as a mom, I wanted to model failing forward to my kids in a healthy way. Every failure is a lesson that teaches us how to do better when we get back up on the horse and try again.

> As humans, we will fail, but instead of letting that define us as individuals, we must reframe our failures as learning opportunities.

If failure has gotten you off track from where you want to be in your life, I encourage you to create your growth plan. Start with the end in mind and write out a plan of practical stepping stones to get you back on track and keep you motivated to reach your goals. As you meet your goals, you can set bigger goals that grow as you do.

When I first got into real estate, I never thought I would one day own several properties, and I'm not finished. But first, I had to create a growth plan to rebuild my finances after my divorce left them in shambles. I created a growth plan to pay off credit card debt and start saving so that I could have a downpayment to buy my first income property. As that income property became profitable, I used those profits to buy my next income property. Manly and I are still using the income from our properties to help us reach our ultimate goal of building a retreat center. The retreat center was not our original goal—it would have been too big to comprehend early on in our marriage—but the smaller successes compounded to make us realize we could dream bigger. I want to encourage you to think of where you want to end up, begin writing out the vision for your growth plan, and be open to letting those dreams get bigger.

> You can reframe discipline in your mind as something that is intentional, healthy, and manageable.

There have been many times in my life when I had to practice discipline so I could fulfill my personal growth plans. By now you know my love of ultrarunning. That took my discipline to whole new levels. Too many times, we are taught to fear discipline because we equate it with pain and sacrifice. While there is a degree of truth in that, discipline is really about putting in place sustainable tools that we can use when we are weak. You can reframe discipline in your mind as something that is intentional, healthy, and manageable.

Discipline creates long-term mind shifts instead of "fad" mind hacks. Mind hacks are short-term solutions to long-term challenges. They will fail us because they are usually extreme and falsely promise shortcuts to success. There are no shortcuts, remember? As I have said before, I don't always love getting up at 4:44 a.m. and going for long runs when it's raining, but I have surrounded myself with accountability partners and a tool kit of things I know work for me to help me practice discipline.

When I am weak and tempted to skip one of those morning runs, I can turn to the coaches in my life to keep me accountable. God gave us tiers of accountability partners to help us through different seasons and areas of life. I know I can turn to my friends when I need people with whom I feel safe being vulnerable and transparent. I know they will offer encouragement and do life with me. At the office, I have my peers I can turn to for brainstorming and to bounce around ideas because we all share common skill sets and are working together toward the same objective. I have mentors I can turn to who will generously give their time and expertise to help me avoid mistakes they have learned from. I have used therapists to counsel me in rebuilding my foundation and heal from past trauma so I can become stronger. I also employ trainers and coaches to help me put action plans in place, build my tool kit for success, measure my progress, and keep me accountable in reaching benchmarks that move me closer to my goals.

It takes a village to become successful, so I cannot encourage you enough to invest in the relationships in your life and start building your motivational team. If there is a specific area in which you know you need to grow, find those accountability partners.

> It takes a village to become successful, so I cannot encourage you enough to invest in the relationships in your life and start building your motivational team.

When I was in high school, I took a public speaking class. I can remember so vividly the first time I got up to speak in front of the class. I was terrified. I made the biggest fool of myself chattering my way through my speech. (And there was a boy in this class whom I really liked and was trying to impress. I was humiliated!) However, that class helped me overcome a severe fear of public speaking. By the end of the class, I could deliver a speech without passing out (and I ended up dating that guy until we broke up two months into my freshman year of college).

That class began my lifelong study of communication. Because of this class, I was elected student council president and given the opportunity to go to my first leadership conference. I learned how to voice my ideas, opinions, and messages concisely and effectively and still use many of those skills when I speak all over the world. As women, we are natural communicators, but we don't always know the best way to communicate in the workplace.

We need to learn to ask ourselves, *Why Am I Talking?*, sit back and listen, keep our emotions between the lines, stay present rather than going historical, use facts and figures to give us credibility and prove our value in negotiations, and have the difficult conversations. I have had so many difficult conversations in my life. I had one recently when I was called into a heated, high-conflict situation. Those are never fun, no matter how many times you're called into them, but I have learned how to ask the questions that get to the heart of the matter. I have developed my emotional intelligence to discern when the words someone is saying are really masking an underlying hurt that they need to address. When I stop to ask the people in the room how we can win with each other and how we can lose with each other, it opens the door for honest discussions that arrive at meaningful resolutions most of the time.

You and I had one of those difficult conversations together about health. Like discipline, health is another tough topic that doesn't always feel good to talk about, but it is so crucial in setting us up to enjoy the fruits of our labor. If you want to be in a position to play with your grandchildren, have an active retirement, travel the world—you name it—you need to make the investment in not just your physical health but your mental and spiritual health as well. God created us in his image and tells us our bodies are temples of the Holy Spirit, but how many of us treat ourselves like the holy vessels we are? You can begin making major changes to your physical, mental, and spiritual health in as little as thirty minutes a day. A physical workout doesn't have to be extreme; it just has to be intentional and sustainable. Just like with our other stones, as you become healthier, your health goals will scale with you and take you to places you may never have thought possible. I cannot wait to run my hundred-mile ultra!

As leaders, not only do we need to be in good physical, mental, and spiritual shape, but we need to have wisdom—the experiential knowledge we have learned to apply in multiple spheres of life. Leaders never stop learning. If you want to grow in wisdom, start praying the prayer of Solomon and studying the book of Proverbs. Examine that Proverbs 31 woman, not as the unattainable standard of domestic perfection she is often described as, but as the real businesswoman of godly influence that Scripture shows us she is. She didn't have to choose between family and career; she got to do both. Her influence was widespread. Today, we can become Proverbs 31 women by inviting God into every situation and learning to use the discernment of the Holy Spirit, by surrounding ourselves with older and wiser women who can pour into us, and by embracing diversity that reflects the body of Christ. He created us with different backgrounds, different interests, different skill sets, strengths, and perspectives knowing that when we work together, we can do amazing things.

> Leaders never stop learning.

Wisdom helps us act with integrity. We don't want our talents to take us where our character cannot sustain us. Integrity helps us to do the right thing even when nobody is watching. When we are stressed out and do not have boundaries in place to protect our integrity, the devil will try to tempt us with small compromises that can all too quickly snowball into big problems. Don't give the devil room to derail you from what God has planned for you. Put healthy boundaries in place to keep you from getting weary and compromising your integrity. As a leader, you are a role model. Your team is looking to you to see how you handle difficult situations. Your kids are looking to you to teach them how to act. Integrity is modeled from the top. It protects your reputation and will point people to Christ.

One of the easiest ways to model integrity is to be kind. #IYKYK. It is just that simple.

Choose to keep your eyes trained on the mountaintop and be optimistic. Just like with integrity, optimism is something we model. You get to choose to expect good things, look for reasons to celebrate the wins in life, and collect those memorial stones to remind you of God's goodness and faithfulness. I had no reason to expect good things for my life, but I saw optimism modeled to me in high school. I saw the opportunities it created because it was infectious. You can choose to see the glass not just as half-full or half-empty, but as overflowing with God's goodness.

> Choose to keep your eyes trained on the mountaintop and be optimistic.

I have seen pessimism, or "realism," negatively affect the spirit and productivity of a workplace. It can suck the motivation out of a team because they pick up on the fact that their leaders do not believe in their ability to perform. On the other hand, optimism gives your team the security of knowing that you have their back, you are cheering them on, and you will celebrate their victories with them. It goes hand in hand with faith.

Faith believes for big things even when circumstances might not reflect that. Faith takes the responsibility off yourself and trusts God to stand in your gaps. You can build your faith by putting God first and scheduling time each and every day to get away with him. I carve time every morning and every night to put God first. I look forward to my sabbaticals because they are some of the most special times when I can hear God speak to me and remind me of my why. My faith keeps me focused on the eternal, the legacy I want to leave behind. Faith is what got me out of the trailer park and broke that spirit of generational poverty so that my kids can do even greater things than I have.

Faith allows me to live with gratitude and generosity, knowing that nothing I've earned in my life is really mine. It all belongs to God. That gives me so much freedom and peace, knowing that I don't have to walk around with closed fists trying to hold onto things. I grew up with nothing. I know what it is like to have nothing. It would be so easy for me to fear losing everything and returning to my days of nothing. But I choose to trust God and be generous. Just like there were so many people who modeled generosity to me from a young age, I want to be that model to others. Generosity not only helps me reframe my mindset from one of fear to one of faith, but it truly blesses me when I am able to share with others.

All these things I am teaching you, I can share with confidence because I know they work. I have lived them. I have achieved success because I have practiced what I am preaching. Each of these stones are taken from lessons I learned in my own life—the high points, the low points, and the pain caves I thought might break me. They are a testament to God's goodness and faithfulness to complete the good work that he started in me and in you.

Maybe you're thinking, *Dawn, it will take a lifetime to become good at all these stones!* You're right! There are no shortcuts to success. But that should not scare you or keep you from trying. You can start today to move the needle closer to where you want to end up no matter how far into your life journey you are. If you think it's too late for you to start working toward the future of influence you desire, I am asking you to test me in these things—similar to how God asks us to test him when we are generous with our tithe—and see if you do not accomplish more than you originally thought possible.

Even if you start by tackling just one of these stones, that is a decision that brings you 1 percent further than you were the day before. Paul encouraged, "Brothers, I do not consider myself to have taken hold of it. But one thing I do: Forgetting what is behind and reaching forward to what is ahead, I pursue as my goal the prize promised by God's heavenly call in Christ Jesus" (Philippians 3:13–14 HCSB). I want to swap out the "brothers" for "sisters" and embolden you to train your eyes ahead to the next aid station.

As I've said several times, success builds on success. As you gain momentum and build endurance, the goals you thought impossible will become attainable. As you grow and manifest those dreams into reality, your capacity to dream will grow with you. You will be able to reach spheres of influence and tiers of success you never thought possible. My journey to becoming a CEO didn't begin when I was a kid. I didn't dream of a corner office. My dreams scaled with me as I became more disciplined in using the tools with which God equipped me in my tool kit. It started with finishing high school—something that many of us take for granted—then going to college and graduating. It took being open to God redirecting my path and taking me in new directions I didn't expect.

J. R. R. Tolkien has a beautiful quote in *The Fellowship of the Ring* that says, "All we have to decide is what to do with the time that is given us."[65] Every day you wake up, you have the opportunity to make choices that will shape your influence, your life, and your legacy. These stones are tools you can choose to pick up and allow to navigate you through your day. It doesn't matter where you were born or the trauma you've endured. You get to choose who and what you will become going forward. You can choose to live in victimhood and get stuck in the past, or you can choose to put in the hard work to move into the fullness of God's plan for your life.

> It doesn't matter where you were born or the trauma you've endured. You get to choose who and what you will become going forward.

You can be whoever and whatever you want to be, but I encourage you, as we get to the end of our time together, to be who *God* wants you to be. Figure out your why, the reason you have been put here for such a time as this. Then you can live every single day as if you are on a divine assignment. I know my why is to be a servant leader, but I consider my job my "assignment." It is my workplace ministry where I have influence on those around me. I can model each and every one of these stones of leadership and let my words and actions point people to Christ.

There are stones everywhere you look in life. These are mine. It's time for you to begin applying these stones to your life and collecting new ones of your own. Build that monument of memorial stones as you move into the realms of influence and leadership that God has predestined for you. Wherever you currently are in your life, it is not too late. Make those choices today! God has an incredible why waiting for you to discover; I just know it. If he can do it with me, he can do it with you. Keep him first and see how he enlarges your vision and your territory.

As we close, I want to leave you with Paul's words to the Ephesians, one of my favorite verses: "To Him who is able to do exceedingly abundantly above all that we ask or think, according to the power that works in us, to Him be glory in the church by Christ Jesus to all generations, forever and ever. Amen" (3:20 NKJV).

Onward and upward! Amen!

Acknowledgments

To God, for his mercy and grace when I needed it and the hedges of protection he put around me so that I can stay on the path that he created me for in the first place (Jeremiah 29:11).

To all the incredible coaches I've had in my life, sports, and business, for showing me that I was meant for more and capable of doing way more than I could ever imagine (Ephesians 3:20). I'm a trailer park CEO because of y'all.

To my Pathways small group: Matt and Brenda Duhe, Robert and Katie Bergeron, Justin and Shay Pohlmann, Renee Huff, Lisa Garsaud, Nicole Landry, and Stephanie Neece, thank you for being fierce prayer warriors for me during all the transitions of job positions, family transitions, and the big move from LA to GA. I can't even imagine my life without y'all (Proverbs 27:9)!

To my Kingdom Business Leaders: Pastor Gary Borgstede, Theresa Hollander, Jennifer Frosch, Carolyn Russell, Denise Howell, Elizabeth Valenti, Gayle Reuling, Holly Bertuglia, Katie Welty Bergeron, Laura Diggs, McKenzie Coleman, Melissa Zornes, Melody Hale, Nichole Doyle, Nancy Livaudais, and Stephanie Turner, thank you for trusting me on our journey to dive into Scripture, learn what God says about running successful women-owned businesses, and being vulnerable and transparent in sharing your heartaches and struggles. Y'all are one of the major reasons this book got written. I thank God for you (Ephesians 1:16–17).

To my Team Navigators: Thank you for eleven years of trusting my leadership to guide us and lead out our mission statement. Thank you to the original founders of our team, Randy Ray, Stacie Ray, Zachary Ray, Heather Oster, and Sarah White. Together we created the mission and vision of our team, which is to navigate success with an eternal impact by loving, serving, and caring for others one home at a time *and* to be a navigational beacon in our community and beyond. Huge gratitude to all those who came and went on our team. You left an incredible impact on our lives and made me a better leader. Yet the biggest thanks go to the "fairies" of the team. The two people who truly made Manly and me better. Stacie Ray (ten years of putting up with us!) and Jill Strain, who is really seeing us through the thick and thin of things. She is the best "work-wife" I could have asked for Manly to have. Jill, you make us better every single day (Proverbs 27:17).

To my aunt and uncle, Fran and Ronny Ussery. Because of your prayers for our family, and specifically for me, God did not give up on his promise to turn evil to good. Thank you for showing me how to forgive and what a godly marriage and relationship should be. Thank you for showing me that God is good (Romans 8:28).

To Stephanie Katz, I am so grateful that you were sitting in that audience when I spoke at SLU. Because of you, this book is written. Without you, it would just be words in my head on a road paved with good intentions to help others. I am grateful that God had a plan and that you listened to the Holy Spirit and sent me that Facebook message that I will never forget. Thanks for running on Diet Coke and dry shampoo. You are the gift that keeps giving (James 1:17).

To Carlton Garborg and Suzanne Niles for reading our proposal and seeing value in a book like this. To Tim Payne, Rachel Libke, and Caroline Rock for shepherding and polishing this from the first draft to the final draft. To Michelle Winger, Laurie Brainard, and Scott Rademaker for getting the nitty-gritty business points done. And to everyone else at BroadStreet Publishing who had a role in making *Trailer Park CEO* a reality. I am so grateful for all your enthusiasm from the very beginning.

Endnotes

1. "Comparing Characteristics and Selected Expenditures of Dual- and Single-Income Households with Children," US Bureau of Labor Statistics, September 2020, bls.gov.
2. Liz Eltin, "New Year, New Glass Heights: Women Now Comprise 10% of Top U.S. Corporation CEOs," *Forbes*, January 27, 2023, Forbes.com.
3. Katherine Schaeffer, "The Data on Women Leaders," Pew Research Center, September 27, 2023, https://www.pewresearch.org.
4. Mark J. Perry, "Women Earned the Majority of Doctoral Degrees in 2020 for the 12th Straight Year and Outnumber Men in Grad School 148 to 100," American Enterprise Institute, October 14, 2021, https://www.aei.org.
5. "Special Topics Annual Report: Women in STEM," US Equal Employment Opportunity Commission, accessed August 31, 2024, https://www.eeoc.gov.
6. "Flight 1549 Cockpit Audio," WLWT, posted February 6, 2009 on YouTube, https://www.youtube.com.
7. "Emotional Intelligence," *Psychology Today*, accessed August 31, 2024, https://www.psychologytoday.com/.
8. An ultramarathon is any run with distances longer than a traditional 26.2 mile marathon. For more information, see Alice Barraclough, "Everything You Need to Know about Training for an Ultramarathon," *Runners World*, February 28, 2024, https://www.runnersworld.com.
9. Chloe Merrell, "First Female Boston Marathon Runner Bobbi Gibb on Starting a Running Revolution: 'We Knew the World Was Never Going to Be the Same,'" International Olympic Committee, May 10, 2023, https://olympics.com.
10. Kathrine Switzer, *Marathon Woman* (New York, NY: Carroll & Graff Publishers, 2007).
11. Jen A. Miller, "Finally Honoring Bobbi Gibb, the First Woman to Run the Boston Marathon," ESPN, April 12, 2016, https://www.espn.com.
12. Susan Milligan, "Timeline: The Women's Rights Movement in the U.S.," *U.S. News & World Report*, March 10, 2023, https://www.usnews.com.
13. Katherine Haan, "Gender Pay Gap Statistics in 2024," *Forbes*, March 1, 2024, https://www.forbes.com.
14. Jamela Adam, "When Could Women Open a Bank Account?" *Forbes*, March 20, 2023, https://www.forbes.com.
15. G. A. Skowronski, "Pain Relief in Childbirth: Changing Historical Feminist Perspectives," *Anaesthesia and Intensive Care* 43.1 (July 2015): 25–28, https://pubmed.ncbi.nlm.nih.gov.
16. Sam Robinson, "Why Are Runners Obsessed with the Pain Cave?" *Outside*, June 27, 2017, https://www.outsideonline.com.
17. Mirin Fader, "Inside the Pain Cave," The Ringer, August 30, 2022, https://www.theringer.com.
18. Winston Churchill, "Speech at Harrow School, October 29, 1941," International Churchill Society, accessed September 2, 2024, https://winstonchurchill.org.
19. John C. Maxwell, *Failing Forward: Turning Mistakes into Stepping Stones for Success* (Nashville, TN: Thomas Nelson, 2000), 2.

20. Robert H. Shmerling, MD, "Why Life Expectancy in the US Is Falling," Harvard Health Publishing, Harvard Medical School, October 20, 2022, https://www.health.harvard.edu.
21. Kat Tretina, "The Average Age of Retirement in the U.S.," *Forbes*, January 26, 2024, https://www.forbes.com.
22. "The Twelve Steps," Alcoholics Anonymous, accessed September 2, 2024, https://www.aa.org.
23. Amanda Westland, "The Hidden Trauma of Overachievement," *Entrepreneur*, June 7, 2021, https://www.entrepreneur.com.
24. Katherine Haan, "Gender Pay Gap Statistics in 2024," *Forbes*, March 1, 2024, https://www.forbes.com.
25. Dr. Louann Brizendine, *The Female Brain*, (New York, NY: Broadway Books, 2006), 22–24.
26. Amy Gallo, "What Is Active Listening?" *Harvard Business Review*, January 2, 2024, https://hbr.org.
27. Justin Bariso, *EQ Applied: The Real-World Guide to Emotional Intelligence* (Germany: Borough Hall, 2018), 9–10.
28. Bariso, *EQ Applied*, 10.
29. Peter Attia, *Outlive: The Science & Art of Longevity* (New York, NY: Harmony Books, 2023), vii.
30. Lauren Medina, Shannon Sabo, Jonathan Vespa, "Living Longer: Historical and Projected Life Expectancy in the United States, 1960 to 2060," US Census Bureau, February 2020, https://www.census.gov.
31. Dan Witters, "U.S. Depression Rates Reach New Highs," Gallup, May 17, 2023, https://news.gallup.com.
32. Debra J. Brody, Qiuping Gu, "Antidepressant Use among Adults: United States, 2015–2018," National Center for Health Statistics Data Brief, September 2020, https://www.cdc.gov.
33. Kaitlin Vogel, "More Young People Are Being Prescribed Antidepressants, Here's Why," Healthline, February 28, 2024, https://www.healthline.com.
34. Ana Gotter, "Visceral Fat," Healthline, January 31, 2021, https://www.healthline.com.
35. "Blue Light Has a Dark Side," Harvard Health Publishing, Harvard Medical School, July 24, 2024, https://www.health.harvard.edu.
36. Aditya Mahindru, Pradeep Patil, Varun Agrawal, "Role of Physical Activity on Mental Health and Well-Being: A Review," *Cureus* 15.1 (January 7, 2023), https://www.cureus.com.
37. Daniel Preiato, Ryan Collins, "Exercise and the Brain: The Mental Health Benefits of Exercise," Healthline, May 10, 2023, https://www.healthline.com.
38. Preiato, Collins, "Exercise and the Brain."
39. "Ocean," National Geographic, accessed September 2, 2024, https://education.nationalgeographic.org.
40. Joshua Brown, Joel Wong, "How Gratitude Changes You and Your Brain," *Greater Good Magazine*, University of California, Berkeley, June 6, 2017, https://greatergood.berkeley.edu.
41. Brown, Wong, "How Gratitude Changes You and Your Brain."
42. "Giving Thanks Can Make You Happier," Harvard Health Publishing, Harvard Medical School, August 14, 2021, https://www.health.harvard.edu.
43. Madhuleena Roy Chowdhury, "The Neuroscience of Gratitude and Effects on the Brain," *Positive Psychology*, April 9, 2019, https://positivepsychology.com.

44 Chowdhury, "The Neuroscience of Gratitude."

45 "Deep Breathing," National Cancer Institute, accessed September 2, 2024, https://www.cancer.gov.

46 "Parasympathetic Nervous System (PSNS)," Cleveland Clinic, accessed September 2, 2024, https://my.clevelandclinic.org.

47 "NSDR, Meditation and Breathwork," Huberman Lab, accessed September 3, 2024, https://www.hubermanlab.com.

48 "Understanding the Stress Response," Harvard Health Publishing, Harvard Medical School, April 3, 2024, https://www.health.harvard.edu.

49 Matej Mikulic, "Anti-aging: Statistics and Facts," Statista, February 28, 2024, https://www.statista.com.

50 "The Biblical Lydia: A Hospitable and Influential Businesswoman," NIV Woman's Study Bible, accessed October 11, 2024, thenivbible.com.

51 *Ted Lasso*, Season 1, Episode 8, "The Diamond Dogs," directed by Declan Lowney, aired on September 18, 2020 on Apple TV+, https://tv.apple.com.

52 Christopher Klein, "Why Coca-Cola's 'New Coke' Flopped," History, September 14, 2023, https://www.history.com.

53 Glen Collins, "Company News: Ten Years Later, Coca-Cola Laughs at 'New Coke,'" *The New York Times*, April 11, 1995 https://www.nytimes.com.

54 Klein, "Why Coca-Cola's 'New Coke' Flopped."

55 "Stop Screening Job Candidates' Social Media," *Harvard Business Review*, Harvard University, September-October 2021, https://hbr.org.

56 Bruce Y. Lee, "Why Kindness Can Be Mistaken for Weakness," *Psychology Today*, August 25, 2023, https://www.psychologytoday.com.

57 Andrew Swinand, "Why Kindness at Work Pays Off," *Harvard Business Review*, Harvard University, July 21, 2023, https://hbr.org.

58 Steve Siegle, "The Art of Kindness," Mayo Clinic Health System, August 17, 2023, https://www.mayoclinichealthsystem.org.

59 Siegle, "The Art of Kindness."

60 Ciro Conversano et al., "Optimism and Its Impact on Mental and Physical Well-Being," *Clinical Practice & Epidemiology in Mental Health* vol. 6 (May 14, 2010): 25–29, https://clinical-practice-and-epidemiology-in-mental-health.com.

61 Karen Matthews, Katri Raikkonen, Kim Sutton-Tyrrell, Lewis H. Kuller, "Optimistic Attitudes Protect against Progression of Carotid Atherosclerosis in Healthy Middle-aged Women," *Psychosomatic Medicine* 66.5 (2004): 640–44, https://journals.lww.com.

62 Richard Schulz, Jamila Bookwala, et al., "Pessimism, Age, and Cancer Mortality," *Psychololgy and Aging* 11.2 (1996): 304–9.

63 Rupert Neate, "America's Trailer Parks: The Residents May be Poor but the Owners Are Getting Rich," *The Guardian*, May 3, 2015, https://www.theguardian.com.

64 National Academies of Sciences, Engineering, and Medicine, "A Demographic Portrait of Intergenerational Child Poverty," in *Reducing Intergenerational Poverty*, ed. Greg J. Duncan, Jennifer Appleton Gootman, and Priyanka Nalamada (Washington, DC: The National Academies Press, 2024), https://doi.org/10.17226/27058. Accessed December 06, 2024.

65 J. R. R. Tolkien, *The Fellowship of the Ring* (Boston, MA: Houghton Mifflin Company, 1987), 60.

About the Author

Dawn Cazedessus is a God-made entrepreneur, businesswoman, and international speaker. After building a successful coffee shop franchise in Louisiana, she found a passion in real estate. As regional director of Keller Williams Realty International's top performing Southeast Region, she now oversees seventeen thousand Realtors and speaks and coaches around the world. In her spare time, Dawn runs ultramarathons. She resides in Atlanta with her husband, Manly. Connect with Dawn on Instagram at @dawncazedessus. For a little lagniappe and all the latest news, visit www.dawncazedessus.com.